YES, I would like to take advantage of your valuable FREE OFFER.

Mail this coupon to:

Dynamic Graphics
Dept. "How To"
P.O. Box 1901
Peoria, IL 61656-1901

Name _____

Business Name _____

Address_____

City _____

State_____Zip_____

Telephone # _____

Type of Business _____

YES, I would like to take advantage of your valuable FREE OFFER.

Mail this coupon to:

"In Praise"
P.O. Box 612067
DFW/TX 76261

Name _____

Business Name _____

Address_____

City _____

State_____Zip_____

Telephone # _____

Type of Business _____

YES, I would like to take advantage of your valuable FREE OFFER.

Mail this coupon to:

"FREE BOOK"
15 Camp Evers Lane
Scotts Valley, Ca. 95066

Name _____

Business Name _____

Address_____

City _____

State_____Zip_____

Telephone # _____

Type of Business _____

Create Profit Building Ads

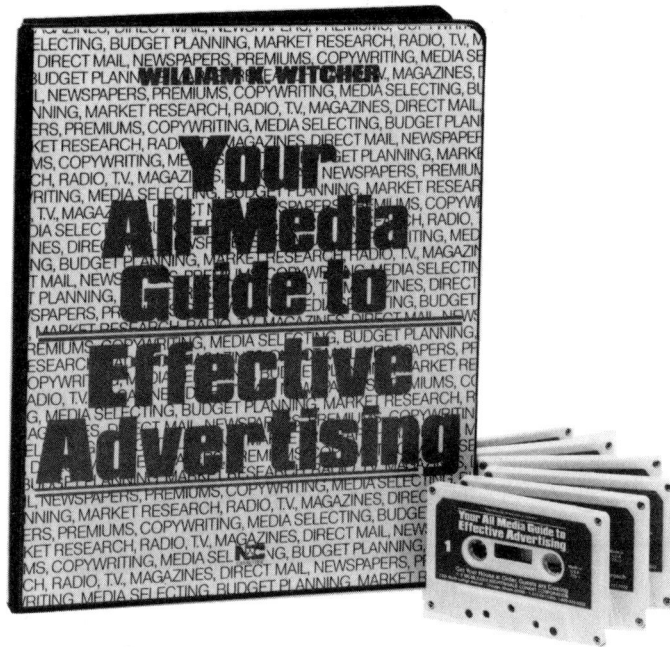

**Enthusiastically Endorsed by
Major Retail and Professional Associations!**

THIS BOOK IS AVAILABLE ON AUDIOCASSETTES.

Bill Witcher recorded some of his vast advertising knowledge on audiocassettes for the Nightingale-Conant Corporation entitled "Your All Media Guide to Effective Advertising."

ENTERTAINING...
VALUABLE...
PROFITABLE!

- special music

- interviews with business owners of all kinds, and professionals in the advertising business

- custom produced, lively, different

- six audio cassettes offering over 5 hours of valuable information to help make your advertising pay

- special discount price
  suggested retail — $69.00
  your cost only — $49.95

- Unconditional guarantee. If this program doesn't help you, return it and receive a 100% refund.

HOW TO SOLVE YOUR
Small Business
ADVERTISING
PROBLEMS

THE ALL MEDIA GUIDE TO EFFECTIVE ADVERTISING

WILLIAM K. WITCHER

MARK PUBLISHING
15 Camp Evers Lane
Scotts Valley, Ca. 95066

ISBN #0-937769-00-2 $17.95

TABLE OF CONTENTS

Section 1

"Get Your House in Order, Guests Are Coming"

Section 2

"Your Customer, Your Budget and Your Creative"

Section 3

"Newspaper and Radio Advertising"

SMALL BUSINESS OWNERS...YOU'RE THE GREATEST!!!

If you are reading this, I am going to assume you are currently in business for yourself or you would like to be. You are a very special person. You deserve all the praise you can get and I am one of your biggest cheerleaders.

Down through the ages the shopkeeper, or self-employed person, or small business owner...whatever term you want to use...was almost like the invisible supplier of our goods and services. If you needed a haircut or wanted a permanent you visited your neighborhood barber or beautician. If your drains became clogged, you called a plumber. When you needed a prescription filled, you simply went to your corner drugstore.

Just think of all the times we conduct business with a self-employed person. How could we manage without Sandy the Florist, or Norm the Grocer or Doug the Auto Mechanic. The Sandys, the Norms, the Dougs...they have always been there when we needed them, but we have never given them the recognition and praise they're due. We have always taken them for granted...until recently.

The most important economic event of the last few years is the emergence and growth of the small business owner. During the past decade, entrepreneurship and small business have moved from a position of secondary interest to one of leadership and respectability. Small businesses, 14 million strong by U.S. Small Business Administration standards, employ 48 percent of the private work force, contribute 42 percent of all sales in our country and are responsible for 38 percent of the gross national product. Small businesses are the chief employers of the young, the old and of women. They provide about 67 percent of initial on-the-job training in basic skills.

Small Business Owners...you're the greatest! I love it when I hear one of my friends is thinking about "going into business for himself." "Hooray!" I say. "What are you going to do? How can I help?" You see, I understand that special entrepreneural spirit that causes men and women to leave secure jobs and step out on their own. I know what it's like to explore new territory. To open your own office, or shop or restaurant. I opened my own advertising agency when I was twenty-three, almost twenty years ago. I've experienced the highs and lows of being "on my own." But at no time have I ever lost that enthusiasm or desire to be in business for myself.

This book is intended to be my answer to the question "How can I help?" I would like to provide you with a basic knowledge of advertising to help you be more successful in your particular business endeavor.

Just remember, you're surrounded by good solutions to your advertising problems. Help is everywhere. The trick is to know how to look for it and that can only come from taking the time to learn about the advertising process. You can't ask for help if you don't understand the questions. You can't differentiate between a good media buy and a bad media buy if you don't know what you're buying. You can't build an effective advertising program for your business if you haven't learned how to effectively use the advertising resources readily available in your own back yard.

I want to stimulate your creative juices and encourage you to learn more about advertising. I want to share some of my knowledge and ideas, hoping that they may spark an idea in you that you can successfully build upon. I also want to remove some of the mystique and overcome some of the fears and negatives normally associated with advertising. I want you to be able to say at the end of this book, "Hey! That's not so complicated. I understand what he's talking about!" I want this to be a positive, enjoyable, and profitable learning experience for you. If I succeed, I'm happy for both of us.

And one last recommendation. Throughout the book I refer you to numerous resources for you to plug into for help and guidance. I would be remiss in my desire to help you if I failed to highly recommend the best instruction manual ever written by the greatest author known to man. It's sometimes referred to as "The Manufacturer's Handbook", more widely known as THE BIBLE. It contains all the answers to all of your business and personal problems. Look into it. It could change your life. May God bless all of your business and personal endeavors and bring you much happiness and success in His Name.

William K. Witcher

ACKNOWLEDGEMENTS

Numerous pages contain "Helpful Information from the Ad Planner" taken from one of my earlier books.

Grateful acknowledgement is made to my wife Mimi who has been a constant source of joy and encouragement for me. Thank you Mimi for believing in me and this book.

Grateful acknowledgement is made to the following for use of excerpts, facts or figures from various reports, articles, books, advertising materials or services.

American Association of Advertising Agencies
Advertising Age, Crain Publications
Adweek
Bank of America Small Business Reporter
Cartoons by Johns
Masters Agency Cartoons Service
Ralph Head & Affiliates, Ltd.
Point-of-Purchase Advertising Institute
Television Bureau of Advertising
Dynamic Graphics, Inc.
Graphic Products Corporation
Letraset USA, Inc.
Dover Paperbound Books
Permatype, Inc.
Monthly Retail Trade Publication Statistics
U.S. Department of Commerce, Washington, D.C.
National Retail Merchants' Association
Radio Advertising Bureau, Inc.
Outdoor Advertising Association of America, Inc.
The Transit Advertising Association, Inc.
Small Business Administration, Washington, D.C.
American Business Press, Inc.
Direct Mail/Marketing Association
Magazine Publishers Association, Inc.
Newspaper Advertising Bureau
Santa Cruz Printery

Bell System Yellow Pages Advertising Department
A.C. Nielsen Company
American Research Bureau, Inc.
Associated Press
E.A. Thompson Company, Inc.
Santa Cruz Dodge and Datsun
Dixon and Son Tires
The Bookbank
County Bank
Seascape
Bay West Advertising
Dunkin' Donuts
Amtrak
The Cotton Industry
United Technologies
The Wall Street Journal
National Premium Sales Executives, Inc.
Incentive Manufacturers & Representatives, Association
Promotion Marketing Association of America, Inc.
Special Advertising Association International
Schonfeld & Associates, Inc.
McGraw-Hill Book Company
National Tire Dealers & Retreaders Association
Tathem, Laird & Kudner
Crain Books
United Way of America
Saul Bass & Associates
NEBS
Potentials in Marketing

SECTION 1

"GET YOUR HOUSE IN ORDER, GUESTS ARE COMING"

Advertising, It's Everywhere!

Advertising touches almost every aspect of our lives. We talk in advertising phrases. One of the most successful advertising campaigns of all time had everyone (including the President of the United States) asking "Where's the Beef?"

It's impossible to enjoy a soft drink without conjuring up the appropriate image that goes with our favorite beverage. I smile when I drink a Coke. And I don't know about you, but I consider myself a Pepper and I think you should be a Pepper too! And come what may, I'm definitely going to keep trying until I catch that Pepsi spirit. After all, I'm part of the new generation.

It's no small wonder my eight year old daughter talks in advertising jargon. When I hug her she says, "Please don't squeeze the Charmin." I request a Seven-Up and she corrects me. . ."Say Pepsi, please." I ask how she's feeling and she claims she needs "Tums for the tummy."

We are bombarded with hundreds of advertising messages every day. . . each one designed to penetrate our inner level of awareness and influence our buying decisions. The advertiser's greatest effort goes toward overcoming the consumer's psychological and sensory defenses, which become stronger in each of us every year as the advertising assault increases. The American Association of Advertising Agencies estimates that there are no less than 1600 advertisements aimed at the consumer every day. Only 80 are consciously noticed, and only 12 provoke some reaction.

Currently American advertisers are spending $70 billion to sell their products and services. This figure is projected to increase to $305 billion by the year 2000. A good share of these expenditures are made by large companies who can afford to spend $275,000 for one 30-second TV commercial in the Super Bowl or $50,000 in research to "test" a $30,000 TV commercial to make sure it will accomplish the desired marketing objectives before spending $750,000 airing it. WOW! Someone once said, "The rich are different from you and me" and Madison Avenue is a long way from Carl's Carpet Store on Main Street, U.S.A. Even though there is a big difference in the placement of the decimal point between your budget and Proctor & Gamble's advertising budget you have some things in common:

- The purpose of their advertising is to **SELL**. . .that's your purpose, too.

- The big companies want their advertising to be memorable. . .so do you.

- They want their ads to motivate the consumer to take action. . .so do you.

- They want their advertising to be cost efficient. . .so do you.

- The big companies want results. . .you definitely do.

- The big company's ad budgets are very important to the media. . .and so are yours!

Your ad budget is the bread and butter of your local newspapers, radio and TV stations. There is room for you in the big business of advertising because you're a very important person. Whether your budget is $1,000 or $1,000,000, you are an important advertising client to someone. Keep this in mind while you're learning the mechanics of setting up an advertising program. Don't be afraid of "the media". Without you, there wouldn't be any media. And besides, those big newspapers, radio stations, and TV stations are filled with businessmen and businesswomen just like you. They have a product to sell. . .they're proud of their product. . .and they work just as hard as you do to sell their product. The difference is that in order for them to better sell their product, they have to help you sell yours. As a result, I've always found the majority of media people to be courteous, knowledgeable and friendly. So relax. . .adopt a positive attitude about the advertising adventure upon which you are about to embark. With the aid of the Ad Planner and the help of your local media reps, you can better educate yourself on every aspect of your advertising program from getting your house in order. . .to identifying your customer. . .to establishing your budget. . .to writing your ad plan. . .to creating your commercials. . .to making your media buys. . .to evaluating the results. We're going to get organized and have fun doing it.

One more thing. . .small and big are relative terms. Take heart, some of the nation's corporate giants began their advertising programs with very modest advertising budgets. Proctor & Gamble only spent $11,000 their first year; Bordon less than $1,000; and do you believe, Wrigley's Gum only spent $30! But Mr. Wrigley increased his budget as he increased his sales. He knew the power of advertising and the need for consistent advertising. Once he was traveling to California on the famous Super Chief with a young accountant from his firm. As they were reviewing the figures for a quarterly statement, the young man said, "Sir, Wrigley's Gum is known and sold all over the world. We have a larger share of the market than all of our competitors combined. Why don't you now save the millions you are spending on advertising and shift those dollars into the profit column for next quarter?" Wrigley thought for a moment and then asked, "Young man, how fast is this train going?" "About sixty miles an hour," replied the young accountant. And Wrigley asked, "Then why doesn't the railroad remove the engine and let the train travel on its own momentum?"

Keep It Simple

Many business people shy away from potentially good advertising programs because they feel they're venturing forth into uncharted waters. They may not understand the mechanics of the program. Or, they may not fully understand the creative concept or the total media costs. In general, they feel they lack the basic advertising knowledge they need to be comfortable with what they're doing. It's safer to do nothing than take the chance of making a mistake. We all have a tendency to avoid the unknown.

However, a successful advertising program is not as difficult for you to achieve as you may think. Advertising is not as complicated or mysterious as some people would like for you to believe.

Structuring a successful advertising plan for your business can be a very enjoyable, rewarding and profitable adventure if you approach it in a logical step-by-step manner.

I'm going to share three basic concepts you should keep in mind whenever you make an advertising decision. . .I'll be repeating these many times in this planner:

1. **KEEP IT SIMPLE**
2. **BE CONSISTENT** and
3. **SELL, SELL, SELL**

Now, I'm sure these three points have been said many times, in many ways, by many different advertising experts, but to me, nothing provides a better guide for you to follow than this:

1. **KEEP IT SIMPLE**
   Who are you? Who is your customer? What is the most cost efficient way to reach that customer with a selling message?

2. **BE CONSISTENT**
   Always project the same image in everything you do. Grab hold of a good creative concept that fits you like a glove and repeat it and repeat it and repeat it in all of your advertising. The competition for the eyes and ears of John Q. Public is tough enough without you competing against yourself.

3. **SELL**
   The purpose of advertising is to **SELL!** It may be entertaining, it may be informative, and it may keep your name before the public! While your advertising may do all of the above. . .its primary purpose is to **SELL**. If it doesn't ring the cash register . . .something's wrong and you should find out what. . .fast!

"RIFLE" YOUR ADVERTISING MESSAGE

You're here and you have a product to sell.

Your message and the vehicle (radio, TV, newspaper, etc.) you choose to communicate that message is the way you reach your customers.

Your target customer is here and he has a need for your product.

DON'T "SHOTGUN" YOUR MESSAGE

Many advertisers take a "shotgun" approach to their advertising, trying a little bit of this and a little bit of that, while not really knowing who they're aiming at or why. As a result, they waste advertising dollars and never increase sales.

Magic, It's Not

The more you learn about advertising, the more you'll realize that "advertising" is not a guaranteed cure-all for depressed sales. In fact, in some cases advertising is a waste of money and may do more harm than good. For instance, you're always taking a chance spending money to advertise a bad product or service.

I once heard a retailer complain about business being bad. To look around his shop, it was easy to see why. The place was dirty, there was dust on the merchandise, two large "Sale" signs were rotting from old age, the windows had not been washed in six months and the sales staff resented customers intruding on their peace and quiet.

His solution to his "bad business" dilemma was to run a "Huge Sale" advertising campaign. For his sake, I hope it didn't draw a lot of people. At least without the heavy advertising, only a few people knew about his poorly run business! With a big advertising push, twice as many people would be spreading the word, "Don't shop at Joe's. . .it's dirty and the sales people are rude."

Joe should have spent the money he wasted on advertising to first clean up his operation and train his staff. The last thing in the world you want to do is expose yourself to a lot of new customers if you're not ready for them. If you plan to invite company over, you should be ready to receive them.

A large amusement complex in Northern California decided to open in June before they were really ready. They rushed their opening in order to take advantage of the heavy summer traffic. By their own admission, they opened six months too soon. And as a result, they exposed an "incomplete product" to thousands of people who spread the word to thousands of other people. . ."Oh, don't go there. . .there's not that much to see!" Their General Manager told me it took them three years to overcome the bad reputation they received by *opening their doors before they were ready to receive guests.* That first impression is so important. . .it can make you or break you.

Guests Are Coming

While working with an advertising agency in the Midwest, I handled McDonald's in four states. It was a tremendous education for me. You can't argue with the success of McDonald's. They are marketing pros. "Nobody can do it like McDonald's can!" They're definitely a first-class example of KEEP IT SIMPLE. . .BE CONSISTENT. . .and SELL!

One of the many things I learned from working with McDonald's was to **check your operations first!** If a unit was having sales problems, either not reaching projected sales goals or showing a gradual decline in sales, they would send an entire operations team to check that unit over from top to bottom. They would re-train the crew, check out the equipment, clean the unit until it was spotless. Only after they were absolutely sure that particular McDonald's was in top shape and could offer the very best in QSC. . .Quality, Service and Cleanliness. . .would they call the promotion and advertising people and say, "O.K., we're ready. Our house is in order. "Let's invite the guests in!"

You can also learn a valuable lesson from homemakers on this point. Whenever we're going to have company, my wife immediately starts vacuuming, washing the windows, dusting, bathing the kids, etc.

She wants everything to be "just right" before our guests arrive. She wouldn't think of having company over to a dirty house. You should apply that same philosophy every day. You're inviting guests into your place of business. . .MAKE SURE YOU ARE READY TO RECEIVE THEM BEFORE YOU SPEND A LOT OF MONEY SENDING OUT ADVERTISING INVITATIONS.

Get Your House In Order

The very first step toward a successful advertising program is to start on the inside and work your way out. Look at your operation through the eyes of your customers. Take an honest inventory of yourself, your staff and your overall business. Try to be objective. Remember, you're looking at yourself as a customer, not as the boss. What do they see? What do they hear? What do they get when they visit your place of business? Do they get positive vibes? Is it a pleasant experience for them?

To help you "take inventory", I've prepared three **Personality Profiles.** These forms will enable you to evaluate three key areas of your operation. Let's get your opinion first. Your employees and friends will have an opportunity to express their feelings on the **Key People Opinion Survey** on page 20.

Remember, as you're taking inventory, be honest. . .tell it like it is, not as you would like it to be. You want to learn from your answers.

**"I agree we have a bottleneck somewhere in the organization, J.P.,
but the trick is finding where it is."**

MY PERSONALITY PROFILE

QUESTIONS	ANSWERS		
(Add some of your own or rewrite these to make them fit your particular business)	Yes	No	Needs Improvement
• If I were a customer, would I like doing business with me?			
• Am I a friendly person?			
• Do I spend as much time as I should with customers?			
• Do I have a positive attitude?			
• Do I like myself?			
• Am I happy with the effort I'm putting forth to run my business?			
• Am I a good motivator?			
• Do I spend more time "smiling" than "frowning"?			
• Am I as knowledgeable as I could be about the products I sell and the services I offer?			
• Am I neat and do I stress cleanliness in my operation?			
• Am I as organized as I could be?			
• Am I good at setting priorities?			
• Am I good at follow-through?			

QUESTIONS	ANSWERS		
(Add some of your own or rewrite these to make them fit your particular business)	**Yes**	**No**	**Needs Improvement**
• Am I courteous?			
• Do I have good self-control?			
• Is my overall business operation getting better?			
• Have I ever mapped out a good, realistic plan of action for my business?			
• Do I know where I want my business to be one year from now?			
Ten years from now?			
• Does the future look good?			
• Do I pay serious attention to what the competition is doing?			
• Do I stay current with the latest trends in my industry?			
• Do I set a good example for my employees?			
• If I were one of my employees, would I want to work for me?			
• Do I respect the opinions of my employees and customers?			
• Do I instill confidence in my employees and customers?			
• Do I trust my employees?			
• Do I provide enough "bonus" incentives for my employees?			

• Do I know my weaknesses? List them:

1)

2)

3)

4)

5)

• Do I know my strengths? List them:

1)

2)

3)

4)

5)

Congratulations! You passed. The above questions were designed to help you see how you perceive yourself. There are no right or wrong answers. Only you can "score" yourself and only you can make the above questions meaningful by deciding why, where, how and what you want to change for the better.

HELPFUL INFORMATION ...from the AD PLANNER

MY EMPLOYEES' PERSONALITY PROFILE

QUESTIONS	ANSWERS		
(Add some of your own or rewrite these to make them fit your particular business)	Yes	No	Needs Improvement
• Are they courteous?			
• Do they project the kind of positive image I want them to project to our customers?			
• Are they as knowledgeable about our products and services as they should be?			
• Are they friendly?			
• Are they likeable?			
• Am I taking advantage of their special skills or talents?			
• Do they take initiative?			
• Are they lazy?			
• If I were a customer, would I like dealing with my sales people?			
• Do my employees enjoy their work?			
• Is this "just another job" to them?			
• Am I proud of my sales staff?			
• Do I make excuses for any of my employees?			

QUESTIONS	ANSWERS		
(Add some of your own or rewrite these to make them fit your particular business)	Yes	No	Needs Improvement
• Is anyone trained to answer minor service or sales questions over the phone?			
• Are they as well trained as they should be?			
• Are they enthusiastic?			
• Are they trustworthy?			
• Do they respect my judgement?			
• Do they feel they're being paid a fair wage?			

Do an employee evaluation on each of your employees listing their strengths and weaknesses. Then make a list of what you're doing to help improve your employees morale and performance.

Your employees are going to be as good as the example you set for them. If you're enthusiastic and excited about your business. . .they'll be enthusiastic. Your employees key off of you. You can either be a positive influence, or a negative influence. The choice is yours, but remember, it all shows up at the cash register!

MY STORE'S PERSONALITY PROFILE

QUESTIONS	ANSWERS		
(Add some of your own or rewrite these to make them fit your particular business)	Yes	No	Needs Improvement
• If I were one of my customers, would I enjoy shopping in my store?			
• Is it clean?			
• Is it a comfortable place to shop?			
• Are my point-of-purchase signs current?			
• Do I tag my merchandise with special "sale" tags regularly?			
• Do I keep my showroom well-stocked with the most current merchandise available?			
• Am I proud of the overall appearancce of my store?			
• Am I a good in-store merchandiser?			
• Do I take advantage of seasonal display possibilities?			
• Do I take full advantage of the many point-of-purchase materials available to me?			
• Do I have a regular daily maintenance program to keep my store neat and clean?			

QUESTIONS	ANSWERS		
(Add some of your own or rewrite these to make them fit your particular business)	**Yes**	**No**	**Needs Improvement**
• Do I remodel my store or at least rearrange my merchandise periodically to stay current with the latest merchandising trends?			
• Do I make it as convenient as possible for a customer to buy from me?			
• Do I have a refreshment area in my store?			
• Are my credit policies in line with the competition?			
• Do I feel my store has a good reputation?			
• Is the exterior of my store attractive?			
• Have I done everything I can within budget to make the exterior and interior of my store more attractive?			
• Is my store bright and colorful or dimly lit and dull?			

A lot of times we can't see the forest for the trees. We're too close to our own operation to notice the dirty floor, or cracked wallpaper or dimly lit corners. Look at your operation with fresh eyes. See your store as your customers see it. Judge your operations as an average consumer. Do you like what you see? How can it be improved?

What Do Your Key People Think?

O.K., you've spent some time taking inventory of yourself, your employees and your store or restaurant. Now, let's find out what your key employees, friends or customers think of you and your operation. It should prove interesting to compare how you evaluated various phases of your operation with how someone else perceives the same thing.

On the following pages, you'll find an opinion survey questionnaire aimed at finding out:

1. What do your key employees, friends, relatives, or good customers think of your overall operation?

2. Do they see your business getting better or worse? Are you improving or going down-hill in certain areas?

Pick some key people and ask them if they'll take a few moments to fill this out. You fill one out, too. Compare **your** evaluation with each of theirs. I think you'll find it very interesting and hopefully, it will identify areas that need improving.

Instructions For The Boss

1. The following survey may be given to your employees, friends, relatives or customers.

2. Once you have chosen your key people, ask them if they would please take a few minutes of their time to participate in a survey to help you better determine your business strengths and weaknesses.

3. Ask them to follow the instructions and give their honest opinion.

4. This opinion survey is designed to determine two things:

   a. We want to know how your company, and certain aspects of your operation rates, and. . .

   b. Are things getting better or worse in each area?

5. After all of your "evaluators" have taken the survey, total the results of each question and divide by the number of people taking the survey. This will give you the average opinion score for each question.

   For example:

   On Question Number 1 —

   "The business in general":

Mary rated it at	3 — average
Jim at	4 — good
Bob at	5 — excellent
	12 = Total of the 3 evaluations

   Divide by the number of people surveyed: 12 ÷ 3 = an opinion average of 4 which is good.

Compare the averages with your personal opinions and see if your key people evaluate your business the same way you do.

6. The results will show areas that are below average and areas that are above average. If glaring weaknesses show up, you will want to take immediate action to improve those areas. Construct a bar graph so you can visually chart your progress to make sure you're staying well above average in all areas.

7. The questions used on this particular survey are very general in nature. When I've used this for my clients, I've structured the questions to fit the business, i.e. restaurants, banks, shoe stores, etc. You may want to take this basic concept and reword the questions so they pertain more specifically to your operation.

"We've been getting complaints about these high pressure methods of yours, Johnson."

KEY PEOPLE OPINION SURVEY

I. Instructions

Thank you very much for taking the time to participate in our survey. We are always interested in improving our business and serving our customers better. That's why we've asked you to share your opinion with us and tell us where you feel we're strong and where you feel we need improvement. We will be asking you to evaluate our management, employees, advertising, products and store environment. Please give us your opinion using the following system:

A. Your basic evaluation on a scale from 1 to 5.

1 = Poor	3 = Average	5 = Excellent
2 = Below Average	4 = Good	

B. The "up" (+) or "down" (−) trend.

Are things getting better or worse in this area?

− = Getting Worse
NC = No Change
+ = Getting Better

Here's an example:

"Please rate us in comparison with similar businesses you're aware of on each one of the following points:

	A. **Basic Evaluation**	B. **"Up" or "Down"**
1. The business in general	3	+
2. Employee courtesy	4	NC
3. Selection of merchandise	2	+

The above ratings tell us that you feel our business is "average", but is "getting better".

You feel our selection of merchandise is "below average", but "getting better".

O.K.? Get the idea? We're looking for your honest evaluation of our business. Your opinion is important to us. Thank you for sharing it with us.

II. Basic Evaluations

On a 1 to 5 scale, please rate us compared with similar businesses you're aware of on each of the following points:

	A. **Basic Evaluation**	B. **"Up" or "Down"**
1. The business in general		
2. Overall management		
3. Management know-how		
4. Management initiative		
5. Management follow-up		
6. Management control		
7. Management courtesy to employees		
8. Management communications		
9. Overall growth potential		
10. Management's desire to be successful		
11. Staff courtesy to customers		
12. Staff morale		
13. Staff training		
14. Overall staff capabilities		
15. Employee opinion of our business		
16. Advertising		
17. Loyalty of customers		
18. Community's opinion of our business		
19. Selection of merchandise		
20. Quality of merchandise		
21. Our pricing structure		
22. Point-of-purchase signs and displays		
23. Interior attractiveness		
24. Exterior attractiveness		
25. Overall shopping environment		

III. Written Opinions

Please list our 3 strongest assets:

1.

2.

3.

Please list our 3 biggest weaknesses:

1.

2.

3.

Thank you for taking the time to share your opinion with us.

Employee Motivation

Remember, we're working from the inside-out and we're still "inside". We'll get to the newspaper, TV and radio advertising in due time, but right now we're still trying to make sure you're ready to receive customers.

While you may think you are in the tire business, or restaurant business, or carpet business, in reality you are in the "people business." People buy your products and people make and sell them! For as long as people have been working together, attitudes and morale have been important factors in the success or failure of a business.

The better you manage your human resources, the more successful you are going to be. There are six important steps to motivating employees:

        1) Set an example
        2) Show them how
        3) Meet their needs
        4) Expect a lot from them
        5) Believe in them
        6) Encourage them

Your employees want to feel they are useful. . .that they are needed and appreciated. A good opportunity to make them feel like they're "part of the family" and an important part of your business is to provide them with an employee handbook. It can be as simple as a two page memo or as sophisticated as a fifty page manual complete with illustrations and photos.

It just makes good sense to take the time early in your relationship with new employees or existing employees to get them indoctrinated properly. Show them how they fit into your organization. Set the standards and conditions of their employment. Your employee manual should be a very positive document that gives the employee a sense of belonging and of pride in the company. Make sure you stress the importance of taking good care of your customers.

WRITING AN EMPLOYEE HANDBOOK

It's not difficult to write an Employee Handbook. Just remember to "KEEP IT SIMPLE".

1. Welcome.

   The opening paragraph or pages are the real "orientation" pages. Give a brief history of your company, who owns it, your business philosophy, etc. The object is to make your employee familiar with his new surroundings and to feel a part of your organization. You want to convey a "welcome to the family" kind of feeling.

2. Some important details.

   After you've set a warm tone, there are certain basic matters that need to be covered:

payroll policies	insurance	complaint procedure
organizational structure	vacations	specific job descriptions
working schedule	overtime	maternity leave
holidays/days off	coffee breaks	emergency procedures
sick leave	dress code	

   Be specific as you can about as many different areas as possible. Put yourself in the shoes of your new employees and try to answer any questions they may have.

3. Taking care of our customers.

   After all the "important details", include a section that concentrates on the importance of taking care of your customers. My personal feeling is that this area need be covered only briefly in your manual because you should be spending a lot of time on a one-on-one basis with your employees emphasizing courtesy, good grooming, friendliness, etc. There is no substitute for communicating in person about a good attitude at work.

   As far as writing this handbook is concerned, please understand that no one can do it for you. **You have to write it!** Nobody knows your business and your policies better than you do. It must be **your** manual, conveying **your** business philosophies and practices.

   So don't try to make do with a manual borrowed from a friend. Write your own! It's not that hard. Besides, writing an employee handbook is an excellent exercise in good management. You'll learn very quickly the need to make management decisions about all sorts of things you might never have considered. It will fine-tune your operation, tighten your controls and help get your employees ready to receive all the new guests you're going to motivate to visit your business with the excellent advertising program you're going to create.

"Keep it up Hooper.
He's starting to weaken.!"

Cartoons

As you undoubtedly have noticed, I'm using a lot of cartoons in this manual. The Good Lord blessed us all with the ability to smile and laugh. I don't think He wants us to ever take ourselves too seriously. We should all blend a little more laughter in with the seriousness of life. A good sense of humor is a valuable asset. I feel the use of cartoons in a publication of this nature or in an employee manual makes the reading and learning more enjoyable. You can convey serious, important information and then make it more memorable and palatable to your audience by following it with a light hearted cartoon.

There are numerous talented cartoonists from coast-to-coast who sell "stock cartoons" to companies large and small at very reasonable prices to use in newsletters, employee manuals, employee posters, print advertising and point-of-purchase displays.

I've had the good fortune to work with two talented cartoonists in putting this manual together: Mr. George Crenshaw of the Masters Agency, and Mr. Al Johns of Cartoons by JOHNS. Both are nationally syndicated cartoonists whose works have appeared in McCalls, Playboy, Cosmopolitan, Redbook, Ladies Home Journal, Saturday Evening Post and just about every major newspaper in the United States. Their work can also appear in your employee manual or advertising for a very low cost per cartoon.

The next two pages give you a little more information on what they have to offer. Write to them and they'll send you a free packet of information and prices.

"Did you tell the serviceman what YOU thought was wrong with it, dear?"

"Who's responsible for this?!"

"I don't know who he is —
but he sells like crazy!"

"One thing about my Alumni Association:
They come right to the point!"

MASTERS AGENCY

For information, write:

Masters Agency
P.O. Box 427
Capitola, California 95010

The Masters Agency offers a complete line of single panel cartoons. . . an inventory of over 30,000 different cartoons covering a wide variety of subjects. Their cartoons are drawn by top names in the cartooning field, including Al Kaufman, John Gallagher, Brad Anderson and George Crenshaw.

"Nothing personal....Nothing personal....
Nothing personal...."

"This sure beats the old lemonade
stand business!"

"How much is the giant Jack-Pot?"

"So we copped a few old relics from the Pyramids.
So who cares!"

35

Communicating With Your Customers

Let's continue along the lines of training. Let's see if it's possible to educate your employees to **communicate with your customers** and by so doing increase your sales by 10%. . .15%. . .maybe even 25% or more!!! How? Through suggestive selling. . .getting more business from each current customer through better and friendlier communications. That's what suggestive selling is all about.

Right now, regardless of what business you're in — appliance store, carpet store, gift shop, restaurant, etc., you have an Average Customer Transaction. The A.C.T. is determined in the following manner: (the numbers used are for example purposes only)

Your total dollar sales are divided by the total number of sales. The answer equals your Average Customer Transaction, A.C.T.

For example, if your total dollar sales for a day were $500 and your number of transactions totalled 100, the A.C.T. would be $500 ÷ 100 sales = $5.00.

The A.C.T. figure is very important because it is the only measurement you have of how successful you, or your employees are with suggestive selling.

To realize just how valuable good suggestive selling can be, following the above example, think what it would mean to sales and profits if you could sell just one more item costing $1 to each of those customers who are already spending $5. Your total sales would increase by $100 and your A.C.T. would be $600 ÷ 100 sales for an A.C.T. of $6. **You just increased your sales by 20%.**

Now you won't always be successful in your efforts and you may have a lot of small transactions. If you had 10 sales at $5.00 your A.C.T. would be $5.00 ($50 ÷ 10), but if you had 9 sales at $5.00 and just one successful suggestive sale at $15, your A.C.T. would be $6.00 ($60 ÷ 10). **That one success in ten just gave you that same 20% increase in sales!** So don't give up. Keep making good suggestions because you never know when it will work. The more your sales people do it, the better they'll get at it.

How do you accomplish good suggestive selling without losing the courteous and friendly touch? Easy. Encourage your employees to have meaningful and intelligent conversations with your customers. Break through the old meaningless sayings we're all bombarded with — "May I help you?", "Will that be all?", "Is there anything else?"

I can guarantee you that if a customer gets to the cash register and your cashier says, "Will that be all?" nine out of ten times the customer will say, "Yes!" and you just lost an excellent opportunity to increase your Average Customer Transaction.

Wouldn't it be better to encourage a little friendly conversation between your sales people and the customer?

- "It looks like someone's having a Birthday Party. . .did you see our complete line of party items?"

- "We just got in some special birthday tablecloths that would be lovely with this gift wrap!"

- "I remember seeing a blue sweater that would go great with that skirt and blouse. . .let me show it to you."

- "Did you happen to notice we're having a special sale on wall paper. . .up to 40% off?"

- "I think we have one wall clock left that's an extra special value. . .let me take a look to make sure it hasn't been sold."

By being friendly and observing what your customer is buying, or by knowing a little bit about your customer, you are creating an opportunity to be helpful and to increase your A.C.T. You're showing a sincere interest and you're establishing lines of communication for a "real conversation" to take place, not just cold and dry standard customer talk.

Even if you don't succeed in adding on another purchase, you **will succeed** in conveying a warm, friendly, helpful image for your store and that customer will be back. The more you try it, the better it will work, and the more often it works, the more enjoyable it will become for you, your employees and your customers.

You don't have to apologize to anybody for trying to be helpful and to sell your merchandise to your customers. That's your job, that's why you are in business, and as far as the customer is concerned, that's why they came into your place of business. . .*to buy something!!!!* The more helpful you are, the more they'll buy and the more often they'll come back because you gave them personalized service. It's beautiful to watch good sales people at work. I've personally gone into a hardware store to buy a paint brush and have walked out with enough merchandise to remodel the neighborhood. My wife has gone into a small women's store downtown just to buy a sweater and walked out with the sweater. . .and a blouse, skirt and jacket to go with it! Both of us were pleased with our purchases and obviously the store owners were happy.

Restaurant Suggestive Selling

While handling the advertising for a number of Mr. Steak restaurants, I saw one particular Mr. Steak owner increase his sales within 30 days by over 30% serving the same number of customers. He did it by motivating his waitresses to suggest an appetizer (shrimp cocktail, steak soup) or a "go-together" item (corn-on-the-cob, onion rings, etc.), with every dinner. When it came time for dessert, his special dessert waitress (all she did was offer desserts from a roll around dessert cart) would come to your table and with a big smile show you the delicious banana cream pie, pumpkin pie with whipped cream, or German chocolate cake and then say, "Would you like banana cream pie or German chocolate cake for dessert?" Almost everyone would look at those delicious desserts and take a piece of pie or cake. The waitress presented it in such a way that there was no question you were going to have dessert — the only question was **what kind** of dessert did you want? Compare that way of suggestive selling to the normal "Dessert for anyone?" line we usually get as the waitress is hurriedly carrying away our dirty dishes.

This particular Mr. Steak owner did a fantastic job of training and motivating his crew to do more than just serve a steak and potato dinner. With "suggestive selling" his customers enjoyed a shrimp cocktail, corn-on-the-cob, mushroom steak sauce and banana cream pie along with that steak and potato. No wonder he increased his A.C.T. by 30% +. Using the same techniques you can, too!

SUGGESTIVE SELLING GUIDELINES

The best way to put together a good suggestive selling program for your business is to analyze your current method of selling and then, using the following suggestions, structure a program that works best for you.

Good suggestive selling consists of four parts: the greeting, creating interest, the close and add-on sales.

1. The Greeting

You want to help your customer talk to you in a friendly and conversational way. You want to open lines of communication, and this starts with the greeting. Avoid lines that can close communications instantly, such as:

- "May I help you?" — No!

- "May I show you something?" — No, just looking!

- "Do you want some help?" — No!

Now what do you do? You've just closed the door to any kind of suggestive selling or any kind of friendly communications. The better your communication with your customers, the higher your sales.

List some greeting lines appropriate for your business that are better than "May I help you?" For example:

- "Let me help you with your coat. Is it raining out?"

- "It looks like it's spring fix-up time at your house! I just got finished last week."

- "I bought one of those and it works great. Have you tried it before?

- "What kind of party are you having?"

List some of your ideas for appropriate greetings:

a.

b.

c.

d.

2. **Creating Interest**

Now that you've opened the lines of communication and your entire staff is being friendly and helpful, you want to help your customers become more interested in your products, services or menu items.

The more knowledgeable your sales people are about the products they're selling, the more helpful they can be. Educate your staff about the quality or unique features of your products or operation.

• "That fabric is machine washable."

• "All of our pies are baked fresh daily in our kitchen."

• "All of our products carry a money-back guarantee. We want you to be completely satisfied!"

• "Those photographs were taken by the world famous photographer Jack Jones who happens to live just a few miles from here."

List various ways you can help your sales people create interest in your products or menu:

a.

b.

c.

d.

3. The Close

Remember the example of the "banana cream pie **or** the German chocolate cake?" The option your sales people should give your customers is based on "which" item they're going to buy, not "if" they're going to buy.

- "Would you prefer the red one or the blue one?"

- "Would you like banana cream pie or pumpkin pie with whipped cream?"

- "That's an excellent choice. I'll wrap it for you."

- "Yes, I like that one too, and I've got just the sweater to go with it!"

Now list some of your ideas:

a.

b.

c.

d.

4. Add-On-Sales

Once the primary purchase decision has been made your sales people have an opportunity to increase the Average Customer Transaction by suggesting another unrelated item. Select some products or menu items you want to feature and develop an incentive program for your sales people to sell those items to every customer they serve during the next week. However, be careful they don't become too enthusiastic and try to sell everything in the store to one customer. If the customer starts to feel pushed, your sales people should back-off. Don't ruin the friendly and helpful environment you're trying to create.

Point of Purchase

Now that your staff is trained and motivated to communicate with your customers, **you want your store to communicate with your customers.** That's right. . .you want your store to speak up and say:

- "Close-out sale on these items"
- "Take me home today"
- "Special Sale — One Day Only"
- "Unadvertised Special"
- "We're overstocked — 40% off"
- "As advertised"

People are normally embarrassed to ask the price of an item or if it is the sale item they saw advertised in the newspaper. They shouldn't have to ask. Your point-of-purchase (POP) signs should direct them and tell them what they need to know. Make it easy for people to get around your store. Use signs to point them in the right direction. . .the direction you want them to go. . .to the items you want to sell. Your signs don't have to be fancy or expensive. In some cases hand painted signs are perfectly acceptable. . .as long as they're neat, legible and spelled correctly.

In restaurants, table-top signs are used very effectively to promote a special dessert or an add-on item. Menu clip-ons are an effective way to promote high-profit dinner specials.

Good POP signs, displays, hand-out materials, samples, etc., can be used very effectively to create impulse buying. How many times have you gone into a K-Mart, Macy's or Sears and walked out with two extra items you had no intention of buying. You just couldn't pass up a great bargain that you learned about because of the huge "20% OFF SALE" sign and big display in the middle of the floor! Do yourself a favor. . .study the big boys and notice how they rotate and promote their merchandise weekly. They're always setting up and taking down new displays and new POP signs, and for good reason.

Ralph Head & Affiliates, Ltd., conducted a nation-wide study for the Point-of-Purchase Advertising Institute based on interviews with 6795 shoppers in 16 mass merchandising stores in six geographic areas. Part of their findings revealed. . .

- 30% of the shoppers interviewed (2010) purchased a total of 3,144 unplanned items, an average of 1.6 items per shopper.

- "Saw it displayed" was the leading primary reason given by shoppers for making unplanned purchases. This reason accounted for 50% of the unplanned purchases. "Saw it displayed" also led all secondary motivating reasons for unplanned purchases. It accounted for 30% of the secondary reasons.

The above information was obtained from the Point-of-Purchase Advertising Institute, Inc. (POPAI). They have many research reports, studies, films and tapes on point-of-purchase materials. Some of these reports include interviews and test results from McDonald's, Dupont, Gillette, L'Eggs, Coca-Cola, K-Mart, 7-11, and Hallmark Cards. If you want more information, write to:

POPAI
2 Executive Dr.
Fort Lee, New Jersey 07024
201-585-8400

They'll send you a packet of information including a guide to their publications and services.

However, all of the studies, reports and publications will only reinforce what I'm stressing. . .

The better you display and promote your merchandise, the more merchandise you'll sell!

"There! That's a good place for my display. . .unless you know a better place I could put it?"

POINT OF PURCHASE IDEAS

1. Signs

   You can create effective POP signs, window signs and exterior signs for your store in a variety of inexpensive ways:

   • Research the various sign making kits that are carried by office supply and art supply stores.

   • Look into the many companies making dry transfer "press-down" or "rub-on" lettering, borders and artwork that can be found at office supply, art supply and book stores. Some companies offering an entire range of graphic arts aids are:

Formatt
Graphic Products Corp.
3601 Edison Place
Rolling Meadows, Illinois 60008

Letraset
Letraset USA Inc.
40 Eisenhower Drive
Paramus, New Jersey 07652

Dover Publications, Inc.
Catalog Dept.
31 East Second St.
Mineola, New York 11501

Permatype, Inc.
14150 Industrial Ave. N.
Cleveland Ohio 44137

Write for free catalogs. These products vary in application and range of alphabets, borders, photos, and artwork, but the catalogs contain easy-to-follow instructions on basic and creative uses of all their products. Letraset also sells Letrasign, which is black and/or white self-adhesive vinyl letters for interior or exterior signs. Just peel off the letter and stick it into place on wood, glass, plastic, etc. Permatype, Inc., manufactures tape letters up to 10 inches in height called Permasign.

Another company that offers a wide variety of price tags, window signs, sign kits and supplies to make signs is NEBS (New England Business Service, Inc.). They're a great company dedicated to serving the small business owner and they must do it very well since they serve over 800,000 small businesses nationwide. They offer all kinds of products that will help you manage your business more profitably. If you're not already receiving one of their catalogs, just call their toll free number, 1-800-225-6380, or you can write them at:

NEBS
500 Main Street
Groton, MA 01471

- Check your staff. You may have a potential artist working for you who would love to show off his or her artistic talents. Just supply them with some poster board and marking pens.

- Talk to your local printer about printing a large quantity of "blank signs" in various sizes that say "SALE" at the top and your store's logo at the bottom with the center space blank. This way you can have a professional looking printed sign with specific item and price information written in the center with a felt tip pen.

- Check with your vendors. They'll be happy to supply you with POP materials you can adapt to your needs.

- Find a free-lance artist and make a deal with him or her on a "trade-out basis". He'll supply you with "X" number of signs per month in return for "X" amount of merchandise from you. Interview two or three artists and look at samples of their work. Normally, there are a lot of artists around, so you can select the best for your particular needs.

- Find the system and format that works best for you and your budget. But remember: *Even a hand-drawn sign is better than no sign at all.*

2. Displays

Do you decorate at Christmas? Why? Because you want to make your store festive, and attract attention, and provide a happy selling environment. If decorating your store does all of that, then why don't you decorate at other times of the year as well. If that "festive philosophy" works at Christmas, it will also work in April.

Use your imagination. Good merchandising displays can be built out of cardboard boxes, old movie or travel posters, your son's little red wagon, orange crates, hay bales, saw horses, etc. Have fun with it! Get your staff and family involved. Make up a series of small displays that follow an appropriate theme or a seasonal theme. Or make up one large display featuring one or two sale items.

The purpose of a good display is to attract attention to a particular sale item or items and to convey the feeling your store is "alive" and "vibrant". The better and more creative the display. . .the more attention it's going to attract. . .the more merchandise you'll sell.

Demonstrations

Have you ever seen a Veg-A-Matic demonstrated live? It's interesting (almost exciting) to watch. Carrots, tomatoes, celery, zucchini, potatoes are sliced, shredded, diced and peeled in a dazzling display of showmanship.

Every 10-minute demonstration draws a capacity audience of people who listen and watch in awe as the demonstrator chops up vegetables in a manner that you didn't think was possible. And what happens at the end of the demonstration? The demonstrator wipes the tomato juice off his hands and starts collecting the cash being eagerly thrust his way.

People love to be entertained and they love to be "sold". After watching, you're convinced that you can't possibly live without a Veg-A-Matic. After all, how could you dice potatoes? You would have to use an ordinary knife. Heaven forbid! How many Veg-A-Matics would have been purchased on the same day if they had not been "demonstrated"? Very few.

Some brilliant advertising man once said, "sell the sizzle, not the steak." A demonstration helps sell the sizzle. It brings your product to life. It makes it real. It educates the buying public on how to use it and how they can't possibly get along without it.

There's a toy shop in the Carmel Plaza Shopping Center in Carmel, California, that demonstrates some of their toys in front of the store. You can always find ten or fifteen people standing in front of this particular toy store watching a clown blow bubbles or fly a battery operated airplane or walk a mechanical dog. A plastic bubble blowing machine sitting on the shelf is not very interesting and very few people would think to buy one. But put that same bubble blowing machine to work and watch it launch hundreds of bubbles as kids laugh and parents smile and you're suddenly **giving very serious consideration to purchasing a bubble blowing machine!**

Demonstrations are valuable because:

1. They attract crowds.

2. They educate the buying public on the advantages of your product.

3. They create a "must-buy-it now" sense of urgency.

Review your products and see if any lend themselves to demonstrations.

Exterior Signs

Look out your window. How many cars drive past your place of business every day? How many people walk past your store window? Are you taking full advantage of this free form of advertising that's available right outside your front door?

Now I know some businesses, due to their out-of-the-way locations or zoning restrictions, are limited in the type and size of signs they can use. But the business owners I'm addressing now are the ones who can, but aren't, taking advantage of the thousands of free advertising exposures driving by their place of business every day. If the only signs you put in your window are "OPEN" or "CLOSED", you're missing a great advertising opportunity.

There is a fruit stand in Watsonville, California, that uses large, hand-lettered signs to tell you that they have "Oranges-10 lbs. for $1", "Fresh Strawberries-$.49 a box", "Iceberg Lettuce-$.45 a head". In addition to all the item and price signs, they have also developed a cute attention getter that reflects the personality of the place. Every week on top of the fruit stand they will place a 15-foot, hand-lettered banner that reads:

- "Lettuce pray for peachy weather." or

- "We got the beet!" or

- "This is a juicy fruit stand." or

- "An apple a day keeps us in business," etc.

They provide forms for their customers to make suggestions and award a $10 purchase credit if your suggestion is used.

Think for a minute — how many times have you stopped to eat at a restaurant simply because you happened to notice a large banner that said "LUNCHEON SPECIAL — STEAK AND FRIES $2.99", or "FREE PITCHER OF COKE WITH EVERY LARGE PIZZA"?

How many times have you gone into a clothing store because they had a large sign in their window that said "HUGE SALE" or "CLEARANCE SALE NOW GOING ON"?

Your exterior signs should be used to communicate with the outside world that there is something special going on inside your place of business. Effective exterior signs let everyone know that you're anxious to serve them. They attract attention and motivate people to take action.

The more creative you are with the use of your outside signs, the more traffic you'll generate inside.

Bounce Back Coupons

One of the most effective sales tools a restaurant or certain other kinds of businesses can use to increase the number of visits from existing customers is "bounce-back coupons" or "repeat visit coupons".

These coupons inserted in each bag entitle the customer to a free soft drink, a free dessert, a free paint brush, a 10% discount or some other special offer on their next visit.

The idea is to give a customer who is visiting once a week or once a month a strong motivational reason to come back more often. Make sure you have expiration dates on your coupons.

There are many varieties of the bounce-back coupon, and if you currently don't have some kind of program to encourage repeat business from your existing customers; explore this possibility. I don't think these coupons should be used all the time, using them just one week out of every month can be effective. Remember, increased sales will come from:

1. attracting new customers,

2. increasing your Average Customer Transactions,

3. and increasing the number of visits by current customers.

You need to work on all three areas to grow and prosper.

Word-Of-Mouth Advertising

Don't ever underestimate the power of "word-of-mouth" advertising — good or bad. Remember the story I shared with you at the very beginning of the manual about the Northern California amusement attraction that opened six months too soon and spent three years overcoming the bad reputation it gave them? "Bad news advertising" spreads fast and when you're a small business in a small community, it doesn't take much spreading to do you harm.

By the same token, good word-of-mouth advertising can spread just as fast and naturally. This is the kind you want to encourage and the way you do that is by asking your friends, relatives and good customers to "please spread the word." "Tell a Friend" is a great multi-media advertising campaign that's being run by a West Coast grocery chain and that's exactly what you want everybody to do — "Tell a Friend". But, you have to constantly remind people to do this. Make it a natural part of every sale . . ."Thank you! We hope you come back soon and tell a friend about us." The very best advertising you could possibly receive is a satisfied customer spreading the good word about you.

Call your relatives and ask them to spread the word every chance they get. Tell your friends at Rotary, at church, at the bank. Try to capitalize on every opportunity. Don't be shy about asking people to do business with you. You should be proud of your business and never hesitate to take every opportunity to "invite people over".

"The Customer Doesn't Care!"

I've spent a lot of time in this first section trying to help you "get your house in order". Far too many business people forget the basics. They forget they need to have a clean store, well-trained personnel, good POP signs and displays, and project a positive image.

Now, I realize as a business person you have a lot of problems. You are dealing with cash flow problems, high interest rates, delivery problems, personnel problems, government problems, economic problems, tax problems and maybe even some problems at home. But, do you know something? As a customer, "I DON'T CARE!" I'm your customer. I'm not your psychiatrist or banker or financial advisor. I'm your customer and all I want is to receive a quality product at a fair price from friendly and courteous sales people. If you, as the owner, are worried and allowing the pressures to get to you, your poor attitude will be conveyed to your sales people. Your sales people will convey that attitude to your customers and your problems are just going to get worse. Before you invite new guests into your place of business — clean up your act (if you need to). And an "act" it is, because when those doors open, "It's Showtime!" You've got to put on a performance that will make your customers want to come back again and again. That performance means smile even though you're tired. . .train your people even though you think you don't have the time. You've got to get your academy award winning performance together or you might as well save your advertising money, because all of the advertising in the world is not going to overcome a bad product, bad attitude and untrained sales people.

O.K., if you feel you've really got yourself and your house in order, then let's proceed. Let's get ready to send out the advertising invitations, because **we're ready to have guests over!**

'Oh - by the way Ruth, I invited the boss & and his wife for dinner tonight. Just whip up a little something."

SECTION ONE REVIEW NOTES

Let's review what we talked about in this first section:

1. Adopt the philosophy of "Keep It Simple, Be Consistent and Sell" in all of your advertising endeavors.

2. Take your own personal inventory. Look at your strong points and your weak points.

3. Take a close look at your employees and evaluate them.

4. Look at your store or restaurant from top to bottom through the eyes of your customers.

5. Review your overall operation and ask key employees and friends to share their honest opinion of your business.

6. From all the information you gather, decide what changes are needed. Get ready to invite new guests into your place of business.

7. Write an employee handbook to help indoctrinate new employees. You may discover some management weak spots needing attention.

8. Recognize the importance of consistent one-on-one training with your employees.

9. Learn about Average Customer Transactions and the benefits of good suggestive selling.

10. Learn the value of good point-of-purchase signs and displays.

11. Take advantage of the free advertising possibilities that some stratigically placed exterior signs or window signs can provide.

12. Remember that people love to be entertained and "sold". Look for every logical possibility to demonstrate your products to create interest and raise impulse sales.

13. Explore the benefits of "bounce back coupons" and other ways to encourage your existing customers to visit more often.

14. Increased sales will come from:

    a. attracting new customers

    b. increasing your Average Customer Transactions

    c. and increasing the number of visits by current customers.

15. Respect the power of "word of mouth advertising" and the benefits of consistently telling friends and customers about your place of business.

Advertising is not a "magic-cure-all" and it could be a waste of money if you're not ready to receive guests. Remember, we're working from the inside-out and now that you feel your house is in order, we're ready to move on to section Two.

"Very interesting, Simpkins, but let's try to keep these demonstrations on a strictly practical basis."

SECTION 2
"YOUR CUSTOMER, YOUR BUDGET AND YOUR CREATIVE"

Who's Your Customer?

In the first section we got to know more about you, your employees and your business. We decided we needed to "get our house in order" before we "sent out our advertising invitations." Now that we're ready to invite guests over. . .

    A. Who do we send the invitations to?

               and

    B. How do we send them? by direct mail?
       Radio? TV? Newspaper? Flyers?

I'll answer "B" in sections 3, 4, and 5, when we talk about proper media selection, but right now, let's concentrate on who to send your advertising message to.

Market stratification, psychographic classification, vehicle audience, target market, demographic characteristic, attitudinal make-up, etc., are sophisticated marketing terms used by large retailers who spend hundreds of thousands of dollars on market research. I'll practice what I preach and KEEP IT SIMPLE by avoiding such terms. However, it's important to recognize that regardless of the terminology that's used, Dottie's Dress Shop in Cedar Rapids wants to know the same thing Proctor & Gamble wants to know. WHO ARE MY CUSTOMERS? HOW DO I REACH THEM? HOW DO I MOTIVATE THEM?

That's the $64,000 question and there are a lot of companies who spend $64,000+ trying to get the answers. But, your research budget is more like $64, so let's talk on that level. What can you do with limited dollars, time and manpower to conduct some research that will guide you in the right direction?

First, understand the definition of research:

Research is a process of systematic investigation designed to develop information to help you make more intelligent decisions.

Market research is the gathering of information on your customers. We view a "market" as a group of people who:

a. can be identified by some common characteristic, interest, or problem

b. could use your product

c. could afford to buy it

d. can be reached through one or more advertising mediums.

Examples of potential markets: golfers, mothers with young children, do-it-yourselfers, weight watchers, dentists, stamp collectors, antique collectors, teenage girls, senior citizens, homeowners, etc.

The more you know about yourself, your business and your current customers, the better you'll be able to plan your advertising program aimed at new customers.

Can you answer the following questions about your typical customer?

1. Sex?
2. Age?
3. Income level?
4. Education level?
5. Where does he/she live?
6. Is he/she conservative?
7. Liberal?
8. Contemporary?
9. Traditional?
10. Sophisticated?
11. Little-bit country?
12. A lot country?
13. Price conscious?
14. Value conscious?
15. What's the average distance your customer travels to visit your shop or restaurant?
16. Write a description of your average customer. Be as detailed as possible.

I do consulting work for the National Tire Dealers and Retreaders Association (a fantastic association that is really dedicated to serving its members) and they just released a "1982 Customer Profile" report.

They sent 30,000 customer survey forms to 1,075 NTDRA dealers across the United States and had the dealers hand them to customers who purchased tires and/or services in August of 1982. The results were analyzed extensively and released to NTDRA members in January of 1983.

Part of the findings showed:

- 8% of a typical dealer's customers live within one mile
- 37% within 5 miles
- 83% within 15 miles
- 19% of a dealer's customers drive 1980-82 model cars
- 33% drive 1978-79 cars
- 48% drive 1977 or older cars
- 83% American made cars
- 80% of the customers are male
- 36% are between the ages of 26 and 40 years old
- 30% are between 41 and 55 years old
- 21% are 56 or older
- A typical customer is married and has children
- 27% have household incomes between $17,000 and $25,001
- 28% have household incomes between $25,001 and $40,000

"RIFLE" Your Message

The more you know about your customers. . .the better you can structure your advertising program. You can "rifle" in on your target market rather than "shotgunning" your advertising message to anyone and everyone hoping that *someone* will read it or hear it and respond to it.

If you knew your average customer was female, age 50+, with a college degree and lived in an area of $200,000+ homes...it would not be a good idea for you to try and reach her on a "rock and roll" radio station with a commercial offering a free pass to a roller skating rink with every purchase!"

Obviously this is an extreme example, but I think you can see my point. If your customers are "a little bit country" then you have to structure your advertising message with that in mind and not use classical music in your broadcast advertising. If your customers are mostly male, then you should have a strong masculine approach to your advertising. Match your message to your market.

Unfortunately, millions of advertising dollars are wasted each year by advertisers who "shotgun" their budgets. They advertise just to be advertising and they have no idea who they're trying to reach, why or how. They're just "advertising"! What a waste. And these are the same people who say advertising doesn't work. Or..."I tried radio or I tried TV and it didn't work for me." I personally know for a fact that advertising works if you present the **right** message to the **right** market at the **right** time in the **right** media. In order to do that you must *first know who your market is! You need to know who you're shooting at before you can hit them!*

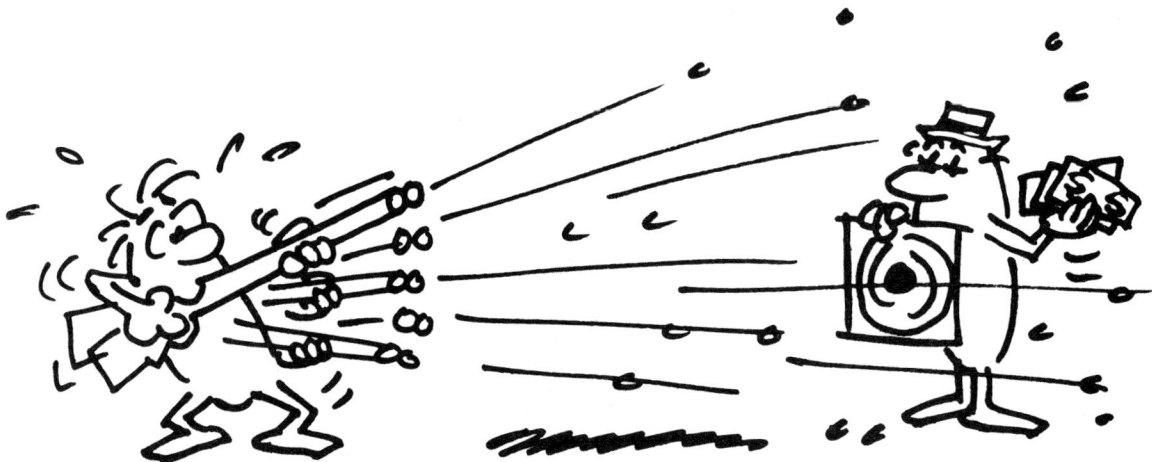

MARKET RESEARCH IDEAS

Now if you don't already know who your "target market" is or you're confused about it, here are some ideas on how you can gather some meaningful market research information on a $64.00 budget:

1. Learn a lesson from Radio Shack. . .they record the name and address of the purchaser on **every** sale (even if it's only an 89¢ sale). This provides a valuable customer mailing list and a source of information as to where their customers live and how wide an area they're pulling from

2. Contact your local college or university and find some marketing students who would be happy, for a small fee or as part of a senior thesis or class project, to design and administer a customer questionnnarie.

3. Contact other merchants in your area who share the same geographic customer base and explore the posibility of having a professional research firm design a report that a number of merchants can use, sharing the cost.

4. Check with your primary suppliers or trade association. They may already have some customer profile information available similar to the report the NTDRA did for their members or they may be interested in participating in a research project with you.

5. Go to the library and do some research on market research. (that makes sense, doesn't it?) An easy-to-understand and helpful book on the subject is published by McGraw-Hill entitled, *"Do-It-Yourself Marketing Research"*, by George Edward Breen.

6. Design your own questionnaire and have one of your relatives or friends collect data from your customers in person or over the phone.

7. Contact your local TV, radio or newspaper rep and ask him if he has any research reports on your particular kind of business. The Television Bureau of Advertising (TVB) publishes a very informative research report called "Target Selling" that contains valuable information on shoe stores, banks, auto dealers, furniture stores, etc. A sample from one of their reports is reprinted on the following page.

TvB
TELEVISION
BUREAU OF ADVERTISING

Shoe Stores
The Best Customer

If you are primarily a **MEN'S STORE,** your best customer is:

	Percent of Heavy Buyers*	Percent of Non-Buyers
Most likely married		
Married	68%	51%
Single	26	15
Wid./div./sep.	6	6
Living in—or near— a large city		
Central city	45	35
Suburban	37	34
Other	17	31
Well educated		
College grad	29	14
Attended college	22	15
H.S. grad	29	36
Non-H.S. grad	20	34
A professional man		
Prof./manager	39	27
Clerical/sales	15	11
Craftsman/foreman	12	23
Other	21	38
In an upper-income household		
$25,000 +	36	19
20-24,999	12	10
15-19,999	20	22
Under $15,000	32	49
Almost any age		
18-24	18	19
25-34	23	22
35-44	19	16
45-54	23	16
55 +	17	27

Source: Target Group Index
*Heavy Shoe Buyer: Purchased 3 or more pairs of shoes during the year.
Note: Columns may not add to 100% due to rounding.

DO-IT-YOURSELF CUSTOMER RESEARCH QUESTIONNAIRE

(NOTE: Rewrite this to fit your particular business.)

Dear Valued Customer:

Would you please take a few minutes to answer some survey questions so we can determine how we can better serve you. We sincerely appreciate you taking the time to share your opinions and ideas with us. Thank you.

1. Are you   (a)_____Male   (b)_____Female

2. How old are you?   (a)_____under 18   (c)_____26-40   (e)_____56 or older
                      (b)_____18-25   (d)_____41-55

3. Would you please assist us by checking the most appropriate response:

	A. Satisfied	B. Could Be Better	C. Not Satisfied At All
a. Selection of merchandise			
b. quality of merchandise			
c. price of merchandise			
d. courtesy of salespeople			
e. helpfulness of salespeople			
f. knowledge of salespeople			
g. appearance of store			
h. merchandise displays			
i. point of purchase signs			
j. quality of our advertising			

4. How many miles is it from your home to this store?
     a. _____under 1 mile   c. _____5-9.0 miles   e. _____15 miles +
     b. _____1-4.9 miles   d. _____10-14.9 miles

5. How many times have you visited our store?
     a. _____1st visit   b._____1 to 5   c. _____6-10   d. _____11 or more

6. What radio stations do you listen to?   (circle your favorite)
     a. _____   c. _____
     b. _____   d. _____

7. When do you listen to radio?

8. What TV station do you watch most often for news and at what time?
   _____ at _____

9. What are your favorite TV shows?

10. What newspapers do you subscribe to?
    a. _____ c. _____
    b. _____ d. _____

11. How much time do you spend a day reading the newspaper?

12. Do you "shop" in the Yellow Pages? Yes _____ Seldom _____ No _____

13. What do you feel are our strongest assets?

14. Our weaknesses?

15. How could we better serve you?

16. Any other comments you would like to make?

How To Tally Your Survey

To calculate the percentage of customers choosing each of the choices to a question on the survey, first add all of the responses for each choice, then total the responses for all the choices to find the total number of people who answered the question. Divide the total into the number of people answering choice (a), the number answering choice (b), etc. Now, multiply the quotients by 100. That's all there is to it!

As an example, suppose in question 3.1 that 68 people checked "satisfied" or choice "a", 23 people check "could be better" or "b", and eleven people checked "not satisfied at all" or "c". Then:

Choice a	68 people
Choice b	23 people
Choice c	11 people
Total	102 people

Now divide 68 by 102 (68 ÷ 102 = .67), 23 by 102 (23 ÷ 102 = .23) and 11 by 102 (11 ÷ 102 = .11). To express your results as a percentage, multiply .67, .23 and .11 by 100. This gives 67 percent, 23 percent and 11 percent. We can now say that 67 percent of our customers chose choice "a", 23 percent chose choice "b" and eleven percent chose choice "c".

Advertising Budgets

No matter what the size of the budget, or how it's determined, or distributed, the experts all agree that you should consider your advertising budget as a necessary expense. Each month you need to pay your utility bills, your rent, your labor, etc., and you should have the same attitude about your advertising budget.

In order for your advertising to be effective, it has to be well-conceived, well-executed and CONSISTENT. (Remember "KEEP IT SIMPLE, BE CONSISTENT AND SELL!")

Far too many business people have the wrong attitude about advertising. They consider it a luxury that can be given up at the first sign of rough times. How often I have heard "things are really tight right now and business is down so we can't afford to advertise for a while!" When do you need the most help? When business is down! When do you need to be the most aggressive to pull yourself out of the hard times? When business is down! If you have the right attitude about your advertising budget, then you won't be as likely to "borrow from your ad budget to help make ends meet" or cut it out all together. In retailing, advertising is not a luxury. . .it is a necessity. . . and should be treated with the respect it deserves. Don't be afraid to establish an advertising budget and consistently stick to it. Remember, the purpose of advertising is to sell. And if your advertising is doing its job, the last thing you want to do is "pull your salesman off the street."

How Do You Establish an Advertising Budget?

Let's look at various methods:

1. **All I can afford method.**

   This is a rather negative and unproductive method. You take a look at all of your other monthly expenses, and after allowing for a comfortable profit, a rainy day fund, and your mother-in-law's visit, you make an arbitrary decision that you can afford to spend "X" dollars on advertising. Everything else comes before your advertising budget.

2. I'll spend when I feel like it method.

Some business owners say they want to wait for just the right advertising opportunity to present itself and then they'll take advantage of it. Your results will match the inconsistency of your moods and opportunities or lack of opportunities.

3. I'll match the competition method.

This has its drawbacks also. How do you know what the competition is really spending or if **they** know what **they're** doing? And what may be a logical ad budget for your competition could be totally unrealistic for you. Besides, you don't want to be in a defensive posture and always "second". You want to finish first and that's why you need to determine what's best for you. . .not what's best for your competition.

4. Advertising objectives method.

Following this procedure, you determine what you want to accomplish in the way of increased sales and then calculate how much it will cost to purchase the necessary advertising to achieve those objectives. The problem with this approach is being able to afford the professional help you would need to structure and implement the program properly. The second drawback is, once the program is designed, it may be too ambitious for the actual dollars available.

5. Advertising investment method.

Many large corporations will "invest" large sums of advertising dollars to introduce a new product or capture a larger share of market for an existing product. They know it will take at least a year or more for actual sales to catch up with their investment. While large companies can afford to do this and view it as part of their normal investment costs, the small businessperson does not have the marketing sophistication, the investment dollars, or the intestinal fortitude to gamble on that scale.

You need to keep your advertising budget in realistic proportion to your actual sales or projected sales. That's why I recommend the following method for determining your advertising budget:

6. **Percentage-of-sales method.**

This involves using a percentage-of-sales formula to determine your annual advertising budget which is then apportioned monthly. For example, let's say after reviewing all the necessary factors, you decide you are going to spend 3% of your sales on advertising. If you're projecting sales of $500,000 then you have $15,000 to spend on advertising (3% x $500,000 = $15,000). You may only have a $450,000 year, but then you may have a $600,000 year. So, calculate your budget on a monthly basis and keep track on a + or − system to see if you need to increase or cut your expenditures based on actual sales compared to projected sales. Adjust quarterly. The budget projection form on the following page shows how to do this.

"My recommendation on advertising expenditures is quite clear — we'll spend what it takes to put the "fizz" back into "zizz beverages!"

HELPFUL INFORMATION ...from the **AD** PLANNER

Advertising Budget Projections for Bill's Shoe Shop

1. Projected Sales for year — $500,000

2. Projected Advertising Budget — 3% x $500,000 = $15,000

Month	Projected Sales	%	Actual Sales	+ or −	Projected Advertising Budget (3% of Sales)	Actual Spent	+ or − Carry Forward
December	$ 59,000	11.8	$ 62,000	+ 3,000	$ 1,770	$ 1,600	+ 170
January	37,500	7.5	37,000	+ 2,500	1,125	1,000	+ 295
February	27,000	5.4	30,000	+ 5,500	810	12,00	− 95
March	39,500	7.9			1,185		+ 70
April	43,500	8.7	(To be filled in on		1,305		(after
May	39,000	7.8	a monthly basis)		1,170		adjustment)
June	38,500	7.7			1,155		
July	35,500	7.1			1,065		(To be filled in on a
August	45,000	9.0			1,350		monthly basis in order to
September	43,500	8.7			1,305		adjust the advertising
October	46,000	9.2			1,380		budget + or − based
November	46,000	9.2			1,380		on actual sales and actual expenditures.)
TOTALS	$500,000	100%			$15,000		

NOTE: At the end of the first three months, sales are up $5,500. That means an additional 3% x $5,500 = $165 can be put into advertising. Therefore, after adding that $165 to the + or − column, the adjusted figure is +$70 instead of −$95 going into March.

Be Flexible

Based on the advertising budget worksheet we did for "Bill's Shoe Shop" I am not proposing that you spend exactly $1,770 in December and $1,125 in January, etc. I am merely breaking it down in this fashion to give you a "guide" from which to work. I feel advertising dollars could be shifted from some of the better months and used in the slower months, i.e., January and February in order to try and remove some of those valleys in your sales curve.

A lot of business people have been very successful in turning a usually slow month into a great month by putting together a hard-hitting promotion. They say they're spending their advertising dollars where they need the most help and as a result have turned a losing month into a winner.

Other business people maintain that certain months for their particular business are going to be terrible no matter what they do. They say it's impossible to create a market that just isn't there no matter how hard they try or how much money they spend. They would like to minimize their losses during the bad months and save their advertising dollars and efforts to capture a bigger share of the market when they know the potential business will be out there.

The choice is yours, but I personally think it is possible, within reason, to "create a market" during normally slow months by running a hard-hitting promotion.

If January is a slow month for you, you'll find the same is true for your local radio and TV stations. As a result, the greatest media buy of the year is TV time in January and February. Your local TV stations will have a lot of highly perishable inventory available during those months at bargain rates. If you plan your advertising correctly, you can buy TV spots in January and February at unbelievably low rates and have yourself one fantastic sale. . . turning some traditionally slow months into big winners. I'll explain how to negotiate for the TV time in Section 4.

I also believe if you come on strong during the slow months, you'll gain extra momentum to carry you into your good months, making them even better.

We'll talk more about where to allocate those dollars and how to write an advertising plan in Section 6. Right now let's go back to determining how much you should spend each year on advertising.

How Do I Determine What Percentage Is Best For Me?

If you have decided that the "percentage of sales method" is the best way to determine your annual budget, then all you need to decide is what percentage for advertising is best for you, and only **you** can decide that.

I know of retail businesses and restaurants which spend as little as 1% and others which spend as much as 10%.

There is no magic number that can be applied to all retail businesses because there are so many variables, such as:

1. **Your location.** If you're in a shopping center or mall you're probably already contributing a certain % of sales to your merchants' association and, as a result, you're benefiting from the traffic generated by the shopping center. If you're near a large grocery store or have high visibility to a lot of traffic in a heavily populated area, you don't need to spend as much on advertising to draw customers to your business as a business that's in an out of the way location. Naturally, the harder you are to find, the more money you have to spend to motivate people to "come find you!" If you can't benefit from someone else's traffic pull, then you have to create your own traffic, and that costs money.

2. **Your competition.** I know of a restaurant which had competition move in across the street. They didn't do any extra advertising or hold any special promotions to combat the effect of their new neighbor. As a result, their sales plummeted by 40% or 50%, and they never really recovered from the blow.

66

I've seen other restaurant operators, who knew they were going to have competition moving in across the street within the next ten months, spend that ten months getting ready to combat the impact of their new neighbor. When the "new kid on the block" opened his doors and had a Grand Opening Promotion, the first restaurant had a bigger promotion and took a very aggressive posture for the first six months his new neighbor was open. As a result, the first restaurant wasn't hurt at all. In fact, both restaurants achieved higher sales than anticipated. The aggressive promotion taking place on both sides of the street generated higher traffic counts, and each restaurant benefited from the other's overflow.

Both restaurants had a higher advertising percentage than normal due to their competitive situations, but it paid off for them both with increased sales.

3. **Change in product line or expansion.** You may have just added a whole new product line. You need to tell your customers about it, so you spend extra advertising dollars over and above your normal budget.

Or maybe you have just moved to a new location, or added another location. You have to let people know about it. Naturally, it's going to take a while for your sales to catch up in proportion with the increased investment in advertising dollars.

4. **Aggressive growth plans.** You surveyed your market area and decided there is a void you feel you can fill through an aggressive sales effort. You want to increase your sales by 50% within the next six months. In order to do this, you believe you have to increase your advertising expenditures by 100%. Naturally, the more aggressive you are in your sales efforts, the higher your advertising costs will be. But, if you have analyzed the situation correctly, your aggressiveness will pay off in increased sales and profits.

5. **Industry Averages.** I think the first step you should take to determine a percentage figure that's best for you is to research what the industry average is for your particular business. I've had the pleasure of working with numerous trade associations during the past few years, including the National Retail Merchants Association, the National Association of the Remodeling Industry, the National Tire Dealers and Retreaders Association and many others, and I've found that all of the trade associa-

tions provide their members with valuable information on all aspects of operating a business. Even if you're not a member, you can obtain their reports and a good place to start is by asking "how much should I spend on advertising?"

Once you obtain an "industry average" figure from your trade association or other source, you can then factor in your particular variables taking into consideration your location, competitive situation, cash flow and growth plans and arrive at a percentage figure that you feel is best for you.

"I take it, you won't loan me the money to increase my advertising budget to buy fireproof matches."

A study of advertising and promotion expenditures of U.S.. corporations and industry sectors for 1980 was done by Schonfeld and Associates, a Chicago-based consulting company. The study analyzes advertising and promotion expenditures of more than 4,000 individual companies in 223 industry sectors. Ratios of advertising & promotion to net sales, and advertising & promotion to gross margin (sales minus cost of goods sold) are also calculated. The following percentages represent a small sampling of average 1980 industry ratios that are commonly used for ad budgeting. However, Schonfeld cautions that within many of the industry sectors, individual companies may spend significantly more or significantly less than the average shown here. For more information on this report and other research reports available, you can write to Schonfeld & Associates, Inc., 120 South LaSalle Street, Chicago, Illinois 60603.

Type of Business	A & P as % of Sales	Type of Business	A & P as % of Sales
department stores	2.9	lumber & other bldg. mat.	2.0
variety stores	2.3	mobile home dealers	1.0
apparel & access. store	1.8	grocery stores	1.1
women's ready-to-wear	2.8	sewing & needlework	3.0
shoe stores	2.2	personal credit institutions	1.4
furniture stores	7.8	finance services	3.2
appliance stores	4.7	insurance agents	.7
restaurants	2.9	real estate	3.6
drug stores	1.3	hotels-motels	2.1
jewelry stores	4.5	retail — not classified	3.5

Statistics compiled by Schonfeld & Associates, Inc., Estimates of advertising to sales by industry for 1980. A & P = advertising & promotion.

Co-op Advertising

One way to increase your advertising budget is through the use of co-op advertising dollars.

Cooperative advertising is an arrangement between the manufacturer and the distributor or retailer whereby the parties agree to share the cost of advertising under certain conditions.

An article in the March 7, 1983 issue of *Advertising Age* dealing with co-op stated, "Co-op is still one of the greatest-kept secrets in the advertising world. So says co-op consultant Gus Cooper, and there are others in the field who would agree with him. What these experts are saying is that many retailers still are not bothering to use all their co-op dollars — the money that accrues to them when they buy products from the manufacturer. But in these hard times, says Ed Zimmerman, vp-co-op development and sales, Advertising Checking Bureau, New York, which administers the co-op claims of some 600 manufacturers, manufacturers and retailers are reaching out to each other as never before to do everything possible to make advertising work and sell products."

Cooperative advertising procedures differ according to the manufacturer, but the basic method involves the manufacturer setting aside funds to be used for advertising. The funds are a percentage of the retailer's purchase or a stated amount per unit of purchase. The retailer is eligible for a share of the funds providing certain conditions are met. The manufacturer may require that his product be displayed in a certain way or the ad be a minimum size or appear in a particular medium. In return for meeting these conditions, the retailer is entitled to an advertising "rebate" from the manufacturer that could amount to 50%. . .60%. . .80% and sometimes even as high as 100% of the cost for placing the ad. The rebate may be in the form of cash or a credit allowance on your next purchase.

Co-op advertising, if done properly, can be of tremendous benefit to the manufacturer and the retailer. The manufacturer is taking advantage of your ability to buy advertising space or time at local rates which are normally lower than those the manufacturer would have to pay for the same advertising space or time at national rates.

You do most of the work. However, the manufacturer will often supply camera-ready ads, scripts, and even video or audio tapes. The biggest advantage to you is the ability to virtually double the amount of advertising exposure you purchase *without increasing your budget*.

Local retailers are simply not taking advantage of the co-op advertising dollars available to them. It is estimated that over $2 billion in broadcast co-op dollars go untouched each year. Ask your local TV or radio rep for a list of broadcast co-op possibilities that might pertain to you. Or write to the places listed on the following page for more co-op information.

"Co-op News"
A publication of Standard
Rate & Data Service, Inc.
3004 Glenview Road
Wilmette, IL 60091

It's the only publication that deals exclusively with co-op dollars and how to find and use them. It's published twice monthly and contains a tremendous amount of information on co-op advertising.

"2700 Radio Co-op Sources"
Radio Advertising Bureau, Inc.
485 Lexington Avenue
New York, NY 10017

A publication put out by the Radio Advertising Bureau that lists more than 2700 sources of co-op money for radio. It includes plans, contacts, phone numbers, accruals and allowances.

"TVB Co-op"
Television Bureau of
Advertising
477 Madison Ave.
New York, NY 10022

TVB is the sales and marketing arm for TV and they have numerous publications on TV co-op. They also sponsor co-op seminars for member stations.

"NAB Co-op Information"
Newspaper Advertising Bureau
400 North Michigan Ave.
Suite 1008, Chicago, IL 60611

The Newspaper Advertising Bureau can recommend various publications that explain the opportunities available for newspaper co-op.

Some retailers complain that the co-op policies of the manufacturer are too complicated and it involves too much work to "figure that co-op thing out!" My answer to that is. . .if someone offered to pay 50% to 100% of my advertising expenses, I'd definitely find the time to learn how to take advantage of their offer. It's not every day somebody is willing to pay half or all of your advertising bills for following a few simple rules.

"She must be in there somewhere — working on our
Co-op advertising allowances. I hear sobbing."

CO-OP ADVERTISING

1. Explore the co-op possibilities available to you by talking to all of your vendors. Ask the following questions:

   a . Do you have a cooperative advertising program?

   b . If yes. . .ask for the details and requirements.

   Make sure you get a copy of their co-op policies in writing and that you thoroughly understand the program so you can avoid potential problems.

   c . If you're told they don't have a co-op plan. . .ask them why not, and what are the possibilities of you putting one together for your mutual benefit.

   d . Work closely with the reps. Normally, they can handle the necessary paperwork and expedite your co-op program. They'll help you aovid problems and maximize your co-op opportunities.

2. Create a form listing the following information:

Vendor/Contact	Projected Dollar Purchase	Co-op Policies	Estimated Dollars Available
(Example) 1. After Six/ Joe Smith	$25,000	50/50 on 2%	$500
(Example) 2. Hanes/ John Brown	$25,000	70/30 on 1% accrual	$250
3.			
4.			
5.			

   Start a file on each vendor to keep track of all co-op info relating to that vendor.

3. After you have gathered all the co-op information necessary to calculate the potential co-op dollars available, integrate your co-op advertising in with your overall ad plan.

4. When you make your media buys, be sure to inform your media rep this is a co-op buy and you'll need notarized affidavits and scripts or ads. They'll do the necessary paperwork on their end to make sure the billing meets the manufacturer's requirement.

5. Make sure you meet all the requirements of the vendors in putting your ads together. Try to "personalize" the vendor supplied ad materials so they fit within your creative format, but still meet the manufactuer's requirements. Show them a rough draft of your proposed co-op ad for their approval.

6. Collect the co-op money due you. The faster you submit invoices and proof of publication or broadcast the faster you'll be paid.

7. Explore all kinds of ideas for cooperative advertising opportunities. If you own a tire store and you're next door to a ski shop, you could work together and sponsor a SKI SEASON SPECIAL on snow tires and skis, splitting the cost 50/50. A home remodeler could co-op with an appliance dealer to sponsor a KITCHEN REMODELING SPECIAL. A movie theater and a restaurant could sponsor a DINNER AND MOVIE NIGHT OUT.

   Maximize your advertising budget by creating co-op opportunities with your vendors and your neighbors.

Trades — The Barter System

Depending on the type of business you're in, you may be able to trade your goods or services for:

- radio or TV time
- newspaper or billboard space
- direct mail services
- printing
- production services
- research reports
- other forms of advertising services

The advantages are obvious. The difference between the retail price you base the value of the trade on and your actual out-of-pocket cost, becomes a discount for you. You may be able to generate $2000 in advertising time for $1000 in actual out-of-pocket expense.

Since radio stations, TV stations and newspapers do a lot of client entertaining, they're always on the look-out for restaurant and entertainment trades. Restaurants, in addition to getting more mileage for their advertising dollars by trading, also benefit by gaining exposure to new guests who are brought there by the media reps for lunch or dinner. So the trades don't get abused, you should put some restrictions on their use, i.e. all tips should be paid in cash, it can't be used on Saturday nights, only "x" amount of trade can be used in any given month and a definite expiration date by when it all has to be used or it's lost.

Hotels, motels and resorts also take advantage of advertising trades. I once had a hotel client with locations in Omaha, Nebraska, and Kansas City, Missouri, and we generated over $40,000 in radio advertising time by trading "Special Weekend Escape Packages" valued at $100 each for radio time. Since these two hotels were used heavily by businessmen and ran at a 97.4% occupancy rate Monday through Thursday and only 52% occupancy on weekends, we in effect traded empty hotel rooms for $40,000 in radio time that was used to promote and increase the hotel's weekend business.

Regardless of what type of business you're in, it won't hurt to ask the media reps if they're interested in trading their advertising space or time for your goods or services. You never know when they might be remodeling or sponsoring a contest and have a need for your interior decorating services, or tires, or refrigerators, or clothes, or luggage or flowers, etc.

Trading, if done properly, can be a very effective way to stretch your advertising dollars.

Creative

In the first section I shared my advertising credo:

KEEP IT SIMPLE
BE CONSISTENT and
SELL, SELL, SELL

This philosophy should definitely be applied to "the creative approach" you adopt for your advertising. I use the term "creative-approach" or "creative" as a noun that encompasses all aspects of your advertising message including the copy, the look, the sound and creative tag line of your advertising. The creative-approach is the total idea you use, and the presentation of that idea in all forms of advertising to help motivate people to take action to buy your product or service.

Your creative approach should do two things:

1. Attract the readers, viewers, or listeners attention.

2. Provide the proper selling environment to sell your product or service.

Grab hold of a good, simple creative-approach that fits the personality of your business and helps to sell your product. Then repeat it and repeat it and repeat it in everything you do that communicates with the public including letterheads, POP signs, newspaper ads, TV spots, etc. There's fierce competition for John Q. Public's eye and ear and in order to penetrate Mr. Public's awareness zone and get your advertising message seen or heard, **you have to Keep It Simple and Be Consistent to Sell, Sell, Sell.**

I'll get more specific about the creation of good radio and TV commercials and newspaper ads in the next three sections. At this point, I want to present the framework for structuring your overall "creative approach."

Let's identify the parts that make up "the creative."

1. The Copy.

The copy includes the main headline, sub-headlines, and body copy used in all of your print ads. It also includes the copy or words used in your broadcast advertising.

Effective copy consists of three basic elements:

a. Customer benefits. The first question a reader or viewer asks is: "What's in it for me?" Select the main customer benefits you have to offer and present these benefits in a compelling way. It's important to understand the difference between presenting "customer benefits" and presenting "nice copy points". Some examples:

"County Bank has been serving Santa Cruz County since 1870"

- This is a "nice copy point". It shows stability and committment to the community. There's nothing wrong with this, but it's not a customer benefit.

"County Bank offers 24 hour banking, seven days a week, at ten convenient locations"

- This is a "customer benefit". It tells me I can bank any time of the day or night, any day of the week at ten locations throughout the county.

The first example seemed impressive, but the fact County Bank has been around for over 110 years doesn't really help me.

The second example definitely tells about something of benefit to me. "What's in it for me?" The convenience of 24 hour banking.

If you could only use one sentence to motivate a customer to open an account at County Bank, which line would you use?

Another example:

"Carl's Carpet Store is the largest and friendliest carpet store in Boston."

- Again this is a nice copy point. Large size usually means you're doing something right and I like to shop at friendly places, but I'm naive enough to expect all retailers to be friendly. So saying you have friendly service is no big deal to me.

"Due to Carl's huge volume buying power, we guarantee the lowest prices on carpeting anywhere in Boston."

- Hey, now you're talking! Carl is going to save me money. He's the biggest volume carpet dealer in Boston, so he can sell for less. "What's in it for me?" Guaranteed low prices.

As a general rule use customer benefits in headlines and try to use as many customer benefits as possible in the body copy of your ads.

b. Simplicity. After you select the customer benefits most appealing to your customers, present those benefits in a simple, sincere and enthusiastic manner. If you get too wordy (I should talk!) or complicated with your copy, your customers won't understand you. If you're not sincere or complete in the presentation of your offer, they won't take you seriously. If you're not excited about what you have to sell, why should your customer be?

c. Sell. Here I go again. But please understand, I can't emphasize this point enough. **SELL!** Urge your potential customers to buy now. the unsuccessful sales man is the one who makes a beautiful, logical, enthusiastic sales pitch and then forgets to ask for the order! Make sure your copy *"asks for the order"*. I've seen so many ego trip ads that consist of an "artsy" illustration or photograph, a fancy logo in the lower right hand corner and one totally inane line of copy that reads something like "For the Beautiful People". This kind of ad is a total waste of money. Advertising is not an art form. If you want pretty pictures, go to the art gallery. . .not to your local newspaper. The purpose of advertising is to *sell!*

2. The "Look"

The "look" of your advertising consists of everything visual:

a. Your logo. (Refer to page 97 for more info.)

b. The type styles you use.

c. The border on your print ads.

d. The way your ad is laid out.

e. Color usage.

f. The overall appearance or "feel" of your TV commercials.

g. The attractiveness or unattractiveness of the people in your newspaper ads and TV spots.

h. The overall presentation, personality and charisma of your on-camera TV spokesperson.

Whether you know it or not, or like it or not, everything visual about your advertising says something about you and your product.

The "look" of your advertising can convey an image of strength or weakness; warmth or coolness; quality or cheapness. We're a very visually oriented society and today's consumer is quick to draw an opinion from just a glance at a newspaper ad or TV spot. Take a close "look" at all of your advertising. Does it "look" the way you want it to "look"? Does it "say" what you want it to "say?"

I saw an ad in the newspaper a few years ago for a newly opened restaurant. The ad had a bold headline in a block typeface. A very strong box border and an illustration of food done in a very contemporary style. To look at the ad, your first impression would be "it's a contemporary, plastic, ultra-modern type restaurant." About a month later, I had occasion to visit this restaurant only to discover a charming, warm, cozy little restaurant in an old Victorian, filled with oak tables, antiques and Tiffany lamps. In no way, shape or form did the advertising match the personality of the restaurant. The "look" of their advertising conveyed a totally wrong impression of what they had to offer. They were projecting a cold, modern, plastic image when they were actually warm, cozy and Victorian.

3. The "Sound"

   a. The choice of music used on your radio or TV spots.

   b. The type of voice, male or female, strong or soft, serious or humorous.

   c. The style of delivery.

This area is covered in greater detail under radio advertising in Section 3.

4. The "Creative Tag Line" or "Descriptive Catch Phrase"

Your choice of a creative "tag line" should tell people about you in one short sentence. It should conjure up a strong mental image to help the consumer remember the product or company. For example. . .

"Nobody can do it like McDonald's can"

"Catch that Pepsi spirit"

"American Express. Don't leave home without it"

"Merrill Lynch is bullish on America"

"Be a Pepper. . .drink Dr. Pepper"

"This Bud's for you, Budweiser, the king of beers"

"When Marriott does it, they do it right"

"Datsun. . .we are driven!"

"Have a Coke and a smile"

"It looks like a Tia Maria night"

"We're American Airlines, doing what we do best"

"Kawasaki. . .let the good times roll"

"Paul Masson will sell no wine before its time"

"Mercedes-Benz. . .engineered like no other car in the world"

"Winston tastes good like a cigarette should"

"Jack Daniels. . .charcoal mellowed drop by drop"

"Honda. . .we make it simple"

"Taste the umph! in Triumph"

"Oh what a feeling! Toyota"

"Weekends were made for Michelob"

"Hallmark. . .when you care enough to send the very best"

"Come to the Sheraton showplace"

Do you have a "creative tag line"?

_____

(Write it here)

How does it compare with the ones above?

With these four elements in mind. . .the "copy". . .the "look". . .the "sound". . .and the "creative tag line", let's review your advertising and see if we can put together a consistent creative that works for you. Here's what I want you to do:

1. Gather all the print ads you've run during the past year. Review them and see how consistent you've been. . .look at your:

   • logo   • use of photos   • headlines
   • border   • use of illustrations   • body copy

Do the same thing with any TV commercials or radio commercials you've run over the past year.

Now, ask yourself:

Are these ads consistent in their style?

Does the mental image conveyed by my advertising match the personality of my business?

80

What do my ads really say?

Do they project the image I want them to project?

Do I list customer benefits?

Do they appeal to my customers?

Do they sell?

Am I happy with them?

What can be done to improve them.

2. If you feel there's room for improvement, then have a creative meeting. Call some of your friends, relatives and/or employees. Make sure you call people who know you and your business and whose opinion you respect. Tell them you're having a little "advertising creative party" at your house and they're invited. You'll supply the refreshments. All they have to bring are good ideas.

Group sharing and interaction is a proven way to develop good insights and good ideas. One person's thoughts and ideas often stir another person's associations, stimulating in him ideas and thoughts which he might not have had on his own. Being in a group of people working together on a problem or "fun project" enables us to work more diligently and enthusiastically than we would on our own. Also, the stimulating effects of friendly competition contribute to greater productivity. Who knows what you may come up with?

Explain your objectives and rules to the group:

a. Our objective is to structure a creative direction for my business which best projects the right image of us to the buying public. We want to tell it like it is; this is who we are and what we have to offer. We want to KEEP IT SIMPLE, BE CONSISTENT and SELL.

b. We need to concentrate on:
   • The copy, featuring customer benefits.
   • The look of our advertising.

- The sound of our broadcast advertising.
- The creative tag line.

And wrap all of the above in one consistent creative approach that ties everything together and best projects our personality.

Should we adopt a
- Western approach -
    "Howdy podner, mosey on in to. . ."
- Folksy approach -
    "Hi, neighbor, our family would like to invite your family. . ."
- Space theme -
    "The countdown is on, we're ready to blast off again to gigantic savings. . ."
- Sincere approach -
    "Hello, I'm Jack Jones, owner of New England Appliance, and I just made a train-load purchase. . ."
- Humorous approach -
    "Big John treats his women right at Big John's Tires. . ."
- Discount approach -
    "Baltimore Stereo will not be undersold, we're the money savers. . ."

c. Here are the rules:
- Don't criticize.
- Don't judge other people's ideas.
- Just think and speak out freely.
- Don't hesitate to share an idea. Sometimes the wilder and crazier the idea the better. It may trigger ideas from other people.
- Share as many ideas as possible. The greater number of ideas, the greater the chances of coming up with a winner.
- Encourage combinations and improvements. Your idea could be combined with someone else's idea to create a better idea. Or a simple idea could be expanded and improved upon to become a great idea.
- Try to think like your average customer. Come up with a creative that will appeal to him, not necessarily to yourself. Put yourself in your customer's shoes and create from that perspective.
- Take notes. You don't want to forget that "great idea".
- Have fun!

Be Positive — Avoid the Negatives

Avoid a negative creative approach. I disagree with negative advertising. I don't feel it's necessary to build your product up by tearing someone else's down.

I knew a Mr. Steak owner who produced a thirty-second TV spot that I think is a very good "bad example" of negative advertising. The first twenty seconds of the commercial portrayed "the competition" as being a terrible place to eat by showing a sloppy, rude waitress; a dirty table with an ashtray overflowing with cigarette butts and ashes; an overdone steak dinner; and high prices. The last 10 seconds of the TV spot showed the interior of Mr. Steak featuring happy smiling faces, delicious looking dinners and in general a very pleasant atmosphere. "Come over to Mr. Steak" was his theme. The comparison between the two restaurants was out of proportion. He spent twenty seconds of the commercial creating a negative impression of dining out, and only ten seconds presenting a positive image.

Look at the mental image the viewer will take from that commercial:
- sloppy waitress
- dirty ash tray
- terrible dinner
- high prices
- MR. STEAK!!!

Is that the way he wants his TV commercials to be remembered? Of course not!

I don't care what you're selling, I'm confident you can find enough positive things to feature that you'll be able to avoid presenting any negatives.

"Accentuate The Positive — Eliminate The Negative!"

Don't Overpower Your Product

Don't let your "creative approach" overpower your product. In the advertising agency business, there's an expression used to describe highly creative people. . ."he's a copywriter's copywriter" or "a creative director's creative director".

I would rather be known as a **customer's** copywriter or a **customer's** creative director. Successful advertising must appeal to your target audience. . .not necessarily to yourself or to an advertising agency's copywriter or creative director. I've seen too many ads, written by talented creative people, that were too "creative"! They were cute, clever or made you laugh, but they didn't **sell** the product.

Here are some examples:

You decide it would be a great idea to dress your six-foot, four-inch brother-in-law in a gorilla costume to sell your "gigantic selection of TV sets" at your TV and appliance store. Or you decide to use a beautiful bikini clad young lady to act as spokesperson for your carpet store.

Now there's no question a six-foot, four-inch gorilla and a beautiful young lady in a bikini will attract attention. The problem is, people will remember the gorilla or the girl in the bikini, but **will they remember the products you're selling????** No! Because your "creative vehicles" (the gorilla and the girl in the bikini) will totally overpower any product they're trying to sell.

The "creative approach" you choose should grab the viewer's, listener's, or reader's attention and provide the proper selling environment for you to sell your product. It should not **overpower** the product.

Remember, your primary goal is to sell your product. . .not gorillas or bikinis.

SECTION TWO REVIEW NOTES

Let's review what we talked about in the second section:

1. Learn as much as you can about your customers. Recognize the need for ongoing research.

2. Write down your personal observations as to the profile of your average customer.

3. The more you know about your average customer, the better you'll be able to "rifle" your advertising message at that target audience.

4. Avoid wasting precious advertising dollars by "shotgunning" your advertising messages.

5. Investigate the various research possibilities open to you from:
   - the local college
   - your vendors
   - your own resources
   - the media
   - merchants' associations
   - trade associations
   - professional research firms

6. Study the different methods of establishing an advertising budget and pick the method that works best for you.

7. Stick to your budget. Don't pull your "salesmen" off the street.

8. For the most part, structure your advertising expenditures to parallel your sales curve. However, recognize the need for monthly budget flexibility to take advantage of special opportunities, unusual market conditions, or an attempt to improve sales during slow months.

9. Review all co-op possibilities and work your co-op dollars into the overall budget.

10. Explore the possibility of using "trades" to stretch your advertising budget.

11. Review the overall creative approach you're taking with your advertising. Review the "copy", the "look" and "sound" of the advertising. Analyze your "creative catch phrase" for appropriateness. Create one if you don't have one.

12. If necessary, hold a "creative meeting" with close friends and create a fresh approach for your advertising that fits the personality of your business.

Now that you know who your target customer is, how much money you have to reach him, and what your creative approach will be, let's move on. In Section 3, 4 and 5 you will learn which advertising vehicles. . .TV, radio, newspaper, direct mail, etc. . . .will enable you to best "rifle" in on and motivate your target audience to buy.

"I've asked Uncle Sam to sit in on our creative meeting to see if he can be as creative with our advertising as he is with spending our tax dollars."

SECTION 3

"NEWSPAPER AND RADIO ADVERTISING"

Media Information

In Section Two, you established an advertising budget. Now we need to determine how to best spend that money. Let's continue the step-by-step process that will ultimately result in your yearly advertising plan (covered in Section 6). Now that you have determined your budget, you should educate yourself about the available advertising media in your area. You're no different than any shopper with money to spend. . .you want the best buy for your investment. You want the biggest bargains and the best media values.

To be a smart media shopper, you have to do your homework. You need to learn about your local newspapers, radio stations, and TV stations. You have to analyze the merits of direct mail programs, transit advertising, flyers, magazine advertising and Yellow Page advertising. It is only through this educational process that you'll be able to:

1. Ask intelligent and meaningful questions of the media reps.

2. Be able to sift through the rhetoric and get to the facts.

3. Speak enough of their media language to understand what they're saying and what they're selling.

4. Make intelligent decisions as to what media buys are best for you. You want to make media buys by choice, not by default.

We'll review the various forms of advertising to give you a base from which to work. But the most meaningful information will come from your local newspapers, radio stations and TV stations. You have to structure an advertising program that works best for you in your local area taking into consideration your location, budget, population, economic conditions, available media, rates, etc. **It's your advertising program** and in order to structure and execute it successfully, you should attempt to know as much about your local media opportunities as you do about your own business. Your media reps will be a valuable source of information. Take advantage of their willingness to help. A successful teamwork effort will mean increased sales for you and your local media reps.

Let's get started on providing that "base of media information".

Newspaper Advertising

Newspapers have been the number one advertising medium since colonial times. The first newspaper advertisement is said to have appeared around 1690. Today they capture 29% of all advertising expenditures compared to 17% for TV and 6% for radio.

There are some obvious reasons why newspapers command the largest share of advertising expenditures:

1. **Tradition**

Newspapers have been around for a long time and a lot of retailers are locked into the newspaper habit.

2. **Flexibility**

Ads can be placed and/or changed on relatively short notice. This allows the advertiser to create last minute ads to promote a shipment of merchandise that has just arrived or run a spur of the moment sale.

3. **Production simplicity**

Every newspaper is equipped with a production department that can take the retailer's scribbles from the back of a napkin and turn them into an ad complete with bold headlines, appropriate illustrations and meaningful copy. The majority of newspaper reps have become experts at interpreting the verbal wishes of the retailer and returning with a well laid out ad. Usually layout is free, but be sure to ask so there are no surprises.

4. Measured results

Newspaper advertising allows the retailer to measure his results instantly. Run a sale ad on specific items and at specific prices good for three days only and count how many of those featured items were sold during the three day period.

Couponing is a very good way to test the pulling power of a newspaper. Create a special coupon offer you desire to test and advertise only in the newspaper. Make sure it's a good coupon offer that will motivate people to redeem it. If you test more than one newspaper, code each ad by using the initials of the publication "SCS", "GT", etc., in small letters somewhere on the coupon. Keep track by publication of the number of coupons redeemed. Make it a fair test. Run the same coupon ad for two or three weeks. Give everyone a chance to respond to it. Measure the results.

Remember, the purpose of advertising is to SELL. You have to be able to measure the results to determine if your advertising is doing its one and only job — selling your goods or services. With newspaper coupons, or specific item and price newspaper advertising, you can measure the results against the cost for running your ad. We'll talk more about measuring results in Section 6.

Buying Newspaper Advertising

Newspapers, like all other media, base their rates on the number of people they reach, their circulation. Their income is derived from advertising dollars and subscriptions.

Obviously, based on circulation, it would cost you more to buy a display ad in the Los Angeles Times than it would in the Omaha Herald. Keep **your** market area in mind when you select your newspapers, especially if you are a part of, or near a larger metropolitan area. It's not cost efficient to buy readers who realistically will not travel substantial distances to visit your store.

A newspaper describes the sale of it's space in terms of either lines and columns or inches and columns. For example, a 3-column x 200 line ad is 200 agate lines high and 3 columns wide. There are 14 agate lines to the inch. The advertiser would be charged for 600 lines. A 3-column x 6 inch ad is 18 column inches.

Column width may vary from paper to paper. Lines, however, are standard. Local advertising is usually sold by the column inch, whereas the same space may be sold by the line and at a higher space rate to a national, or out-of-area advertiser. Be sure you are being charged the local rates.

"Bigger" in newspaper advertising does not **always** bring an equally bigger return. The larger your ad, the more likely it will be noticed, but not necessarily in proportion to the increased cost. For example, one way to stretch your advertising dollars is to take a good look at the difference between a 25-column inch ad and a 20-column inch ad. By shaving your ads a few inches, you will save money allowing for greater frequency or the ability to run a larger special promotion ad later on. And if your ad is well-thought-out and well-laid-out, reducing it by a few inches, should not hurt its effectiveness. You're sacrificing a little on the size of the ad to gain more frequency within the same budget limitations.

Most newspapers offer discounts for advertising in bulk. . .for weekly or monthly frequency, for a contracted yearly quantity, for full pages or "double trucks" (two adjacent full pages). When two or more local publications are under the same ownership, there is often a combination or "pick up" rate to encourage you to advertise in both papers. There are different rates for political, entertainment or religious advertising. There are different rates for tabloids. Some papers charge a "position" or premium rate for placing your ad in a particular section or page. An additional charge is made for each color added to an ad.

Some newspaper rate cards are very easy to understand. They indicate a rate per column inch by business category for varying quantities of usage. If you want to use color in your ad, there is a flat charge. They're simple, easy-to-understand and to the point.

Other newspaper rate cards are so complicated and have so many variables that it takes a degree in accounting with post-graduate work in hieroglyphics to decipher them. Someday, perhaps, all newspapers will follow my advertising philosophy...KEEP IT SIMPLE, BE CONSISTENT and SELL! But, until that time, you're going to have to rely on your local newspaper reps to explain their rate cards to you in detail. Take your time, listen carefully and ask a lot of questions. Learn all the variables and decide what type of contract is best for you.

I have put together the following Ad Planner Information Form to help you keep track of your newspaper rates. Copy the form and fill out one for each newspaper. Your ad size will probably fall within those I've outlined. If it doesn't, use this as a guide and make your own form.

"The newspaper wants cash in advance before they'll run our 'HELP WANTED' ad."

NEWSPAPER RATES
INFORMATION FORM

Name of Newspaper _____

My Rep _____ Phone #_____

Address _____

City, State and Zip _____

The following rate is based upon my contracted rate for the amount of inches noted:

My per inch rate is_____based on_____inches per month/year.

My contract runs from_____to_____.

Add $_____per color per ad.

Full Page   = _____ inches x $_____ per inch = $_____

Half Page   = _____ inches x $_____ per inch = $_____

One Third Page   = _____ inches x $_____ per inch = $_____

Quarter Page   = _____ inches x $_____ per inch = $_____

One Eighth Page = _____ inches x $_____ per inch = $_____

The Essentials of an Effective Newspaper Ad

The National Retail Merchants Association publishes a planbook every September for use during the following year. It's called the "Marketing — Sales Promotion — Advertising Planbook". It is a valuable planning tool that contains all sorts of information, charts, graphs, calendars, forms, etc., and is well worth the $7.50 member price or $10.25 non-member price. If you would like to obtain one of these just write to:

> National Retail Merchants Association
> Sales Promotion Division
> 100 West 31st Street
> New York, New York 10001

With their permission, I would like to share what they have to say about "The Essentials of Effective Newspaper Advertising":

Over a period of years many studies have been done on position, timing and creativity in newspaper advertising. The results of these tests show that:

A. In general there is no significant variation in ad reading by

   Month of year

   Day of week

   Back of section vs. inside

   Position on page

B. Editorial and ad content can make a significant difference in ad performance.

C. Readership increases with ad size, but not proportionately. Bigger ads reach more of potential prospects in addition to immediate prospects.

D. Ad performance is strongly affected by color. Even the addition of one color can increase ad rating up to 50%.

E. Creativity can double ad performance.

The following suggestions for copy and layout can increase readership and inspire creativity.

1. Make your ads easily recognizable.

Studies have shown that advertisements which are distinctive in their use of art, layout techniques and type faces usually enjoy a higher readership than run-of-the-mill advertising. Try to make your ads distinctively different in appearance from the advertising of your competitors and then keep your ads' appearance **CONSISTENT.** This way, readers will recognize your ads even before they read them.

2. Use a simple layout.

Ads should not be crossword puzzles. The layout should carry the reader's eye through the message easily and in proper sequence: from headline to illustration to explanatory copy to price to your store's name. Avoid the use of too many different type faces, overly decorative borders and reverse plates. All of these devices are distracting and will reduce the number of readers who receive your entire message. (KEEP IT SIMPLE!)

3. Use a dominant element.

Use a large picture or headline to insure quick visibility. Photographs and realistic drawings have about equal attention-getting value, but photographs of real people enjoy more readership. So do action pictures. Photographs of local people or places also have high attention value. Use good art work. It will pay off in extra readership.

4. Use a prominent "benefit headline".

The first question a reader asks of an ad is: "What's in it for me?" Select the main benefit which your merchandise offers and feature it in a compelling headline. Amplify this message in subheads. Remember that "label" headlines do little selling. Always try to appeal to one or more of the basic desires of your readers: safety, fun, leisure, health, beauty, thrift, popularity. "How to" headlines encourage full copy readership, as do headlines which include specific information or helpful suggestions. Avoid generalized quality claims. Your headline will be easier to read if it is black on white and is not surprinted on part of the illustration.

5. Let your white space work for you.

Don't overcrowd your ad. White space is an important layout element in newspaper advertising because the average page is so heavy with small type. White space focuses the reader's attention on your ad and will make your headline and illustration stand out. When a "crowded" ad is necessary, such as for a sale, departmentalize your items so that the reader can find his way through them easily.

6. Make your copy complete.

Know all there is to know about the merchandise you sell and select the benefits most appealing to your customers. These benefits might have to do with fashion, design, performance or the construction of your merchandise. Sizes and colors available are important, pertinent information. Your copy should be enthusiastic, sincere. A block of copy written in complete sentences is easier to read than one composed of phrases and random words.

7. State price or range of prices.

Dollar figures have good attention value. Don't be afraid to quote your price, even if it's high. Readers often will overestimate omitted prices. If the advertised price is high, explain why the item represents a good value, perhaps because of superior materials or workmanship, or extra luxury features. If the price is low, support it with factual statements which create belief, such as information on your closeout sale, special purchase or clearance. Point out the actual savings to the reader and spell out your credit and layaway plans.

8. Urge your readers to buy now.

Ask for the sale. You can stimulate prompt action by using such phrases as "limited supply" or "this week only." If mail-order coupons are included in your ads, provide spaces large enough for customers to fill them in easily.

AND A FEW DON'TS. . .

Don't forget your store name and address.

Check every ad to be certain you have included your store name, address, telephone number and store hours. Even if yours is a long-established store, this is important. New families move into your market every day.

Don't be too clever.

Many people distrust cleverness in advertising, just as they distrust sales men who are too glib. Headlines and copy generally are far more effective when they are straightforward than when they are tricky. Clever or tricky headlines and copy often are misunderstood.

Don't use unusual or difficult words.

Many of your customers may not understand words which are familiar to you. Words like "courturier", "gourmet", "coiffure", as well as trade and technical terms, may be confusing and misunderstood. Everybody understands **simple** language. Use it.

Don't generalize.

Be specific at all times. Shoppers want all the facts before they buy. Don't say "comes in the latest fashion colors" be specific — blue, mauve, yellow.

Don't make excessive claims.

The surest way to lose customers is to make claims in your advertising that you can't back up in your store. Go easy with superlatives and unbelievable values. Remember: if you claim your prices are unbelievable, your readers are likely to agree.

Producing Good Newspaper Ads

I'm very pleased that The National Retail Merchant's Association confirms my philosophy of "KEEP IT SIMPLE, BE CONSISTENT and SELL."

Now, where do you find the help you need to produce effective newspaper ads? There are a lot of possibilities open to you:

1. **Let the newspaper do it.**

   You can "rough out" the general idea for your newspaper ad on a plain sheet of paper and your sales rep will take it to his production department. They'll revise it, add appropriate illustrations, improve upon your original idea and send back a nice looking newspaper ad. Make sure you ask for a "proof" before the ad is run. Without question this is the simplest, most inexpensive way to get your newspaper ads produced. The only drawback is the typical newspaper production department is very busy. They can't afford to spend a great deal of time creating your particular ad. As a result, there is a chance your ad will have basically the same look as some other ads.

2. **Hire a free-lance artist.**

There are many free-lance artists around who would welcome the opportunity to work with you on an hourly rate for cash or perhaps trade, or a combination of both, to create your newspaper advertising. Depending upon the qualifications of the artist, he may be able to design your ad, shoot any necessary photos, do appropriate illustrations, get the type set or instruct the newspaper as to the kind and size of type he wants and in general give you a finished ad ready to go to the newspaper.

Obviously, this kind of service would cost you more than if the newspaper did all the work, but you'd be surprised how many talented free-lance artists are looking for work and are willing to give high quality art services for comparatively low costs. The advantage to this approach is that you will be able to develop newspaper ads *that are distinctively yours.* Hopefully, by working closely with you, the free-lance artist you choose will be able to capture the true personality of your store and convey that personality in all of the print ads. Remember, one of the main reasons you're hiring an artist is to give your advertising a distinctive look. . .to make it "stand out". Another advantage of working with a free-lance artist is he may be able to help you with your POP signs and displays.

3. **Hire an advertising agency.**

We'll discuss this possibility in Section 6. If your advertising budget is large enough to warrant an advertising agency, you will want them to get totally involved in all phases of your marketing program, including the creation of your newspaper ads or at least the basic creative format you'll follow.

4. **Do it yourself.**

If you've got the time and the creative inclination, there is no reason why you can't write and produce your own newspaper ads.

The following pages have some helpful hints to aid you in this endeavor.

a. **Logo**

For three years, I had the pleasure of serving as Vice President and Director of Public Relations for the United Way of Santa Cruz County. In that capacity, I attended numerous United Way Public Relations Seminars and had the opportunity to see a film and read about the creation of the United Way logo by internationally-known communication consultants, Saul Bass & Associates.

In regard to the importance of having a consistent advertising approach, Saul Bass said:

"A comprehensive communication approach is one that uses every medium of communication to its optimum in reaching audiences. It is a balanced approach that has continuity between its separate parts. An approach that standardizes its message to obtain maximum exposure through repetition; and that uses the most effective tools and techniques available. Its effectiveness is measured in its ability to inform, to educate and to motivate people. The vehicle by which visual communication problems are sorted out, defined and remedied is called a graphic identity program. A key element of that program is your logo."

A logo is your store's name or graphic symbol presented in a special lettering style, typeface or illustration and used as your company's identifying symbol in the manner of a service mark.

The United Way logo was carefully and thoughtfully designed to convey United Way as a contemporary organization, sensitive to the changing needs of our society. To graphically depict the intent of the organization, man was placed at the center of the symbol, supported by a helping hand beneath a rainbow, symbolic of the hope and promise that is made possible because there is a United Way. It is a strong and compelling graphic device, instantly identifying any communication as "United Way".

A good logo is your "stamp of approval". It's your company's signature and a vital element toward achieving consistency in all of your advertising. Your logo should tell a story about you. It should reflect your company's personality. If you don't already have a good company logo. . .get one made and then use it on all of your advertising.

LOGO SAMPLES

b. Border

In addition to the consistency offered by a distinctive logo, you will also want to try to achieve some kind of special look for your ads by the kind of border you choose. Your logo and border should be the same in every ad you run. They will provide the consistent "look" to your ads that will keep you from competing against yourself by constantly changing your ads. Once you have your logo and border format established, it's merely a matter of "dropping in" the appropriate illustrations and copy points for the rest of your ad.

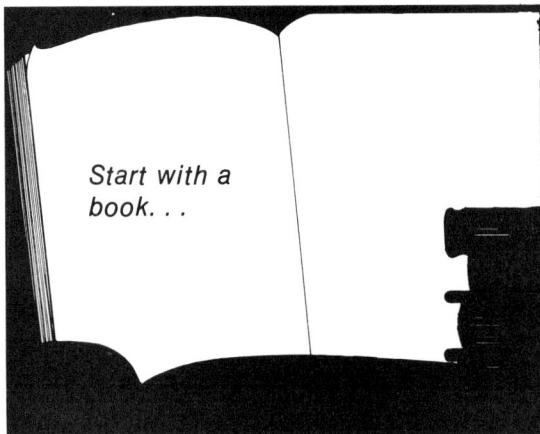

Start with a book. . .

Add a coffee mug. . .

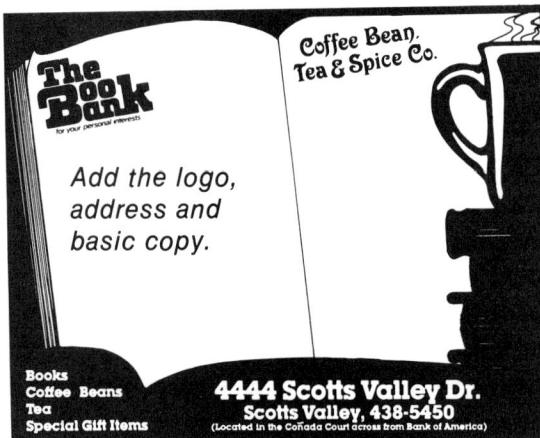

This becomes your standard format.

Drop in the body copy that can change as necessary.

Here's an example of using your "logo" as the border for your newspaper ads.

Basic Logo

The logo is split in half, and the center section is filled with copy that can change as often as you want.

Seascape
SPECIAL
THANKSGIVING BUFFET
choice of
ROAST LEG OF LAMB with hot mint sauce
ROAST TURKEY with dressing
BAKED SMOKED HAM GLACE   7.75
DINNER MENU
served from 2:00 until 9:00
our special salad with croutons and shrimp
choice of dressing
choice of rice pilaf or baked potato
ROAST PRIME RIB OF BEEF 11.95
TOP SIRLOIN STEAK 9.95
thick cut with mushroom crown
FILET OF SOLE, ALMONDINE 7.95
SEAFOOD MARGUERITE 9.50
(Prawns, Sole, Scallops, Oysters)
Includes choice of desserts
Sherbert/Ice Cream/Pumpkin Pie with Whipped Cream
Mince meat with Hot Brandy Sauce
COFFEE — TEA — MILK
CHILD'S BUFFET (under 10) 5.25
reservations suggested
610 Clubhouse Drive, Aptos, Ca.
(408) 688-3254
From HWY 1, take Rio Del Mar exit to the golf course.
The Good Life...On Monterey Bay

c. **Illustraions**

Many of your vendors can provide you with ad slicks showing the merchandise you'll want to feature. What you don't have in your files, the newspaper can probably provide.

In addition to product shots, you'll also need some appropriate illustrations for certain holiday themes or sales, i.e., Washington's Birthday, Clearance Sale, Christmas, Overstocked Sale, etc. Dynamic Graphics in Peoria, Illinois, offers two camera-ready art services. . . Clipper Creative Art Service and PMS (Print Media Service). They provide high quality, professional art for a fraction of the cost of custom produced material. In addition to providing a virtually unlimited assortment of creative art elements, they also offer page after page of suggested layouts, idea starters, demonstrations and crisp, well-written copy. All art is line work and easily converted to two or more colors.

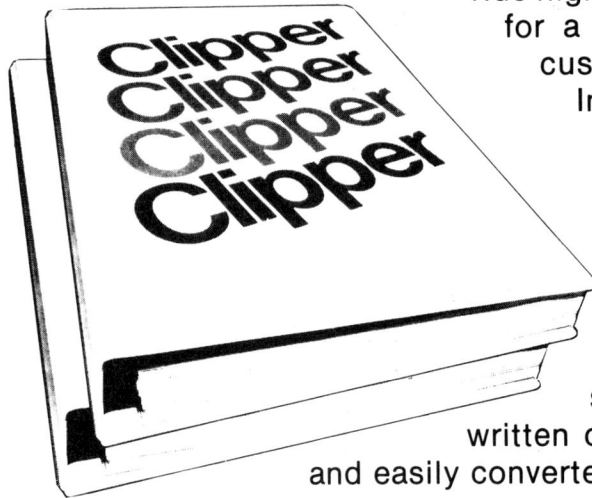

Both services are very modestly priced considering the quantity and high quality of the art work provided. Subject matter is timed to arrive on the subscribers desk a couple of months ahead of a holiday or seasonal promotion. For example, 4th of July material will go into the mail during May. Christmas is sent during October. You can also use their art elements to make attractive POP signs and displays, direct mail pieces, and internal employee handbooks and memos. For more information about their services, write or call for a free catalog:

Dynamic Graphics
P.O. Box 1901
Peoria, Illinois 61656
(309) 691-0428

Clip-art sheets as received from Dynamic Graphics:

Dover Paperbound books, found in most bookstores, carry a wide range of graphics books for under $5.00. These books vary from how-to books on lettering and layout to books of designs, borders, photos and old time woodcuts. They carry a wide assortment of camera ready art-cuts from Renaissance on up to present day styles.

Free catalogs are available by writing:
Dept. DA
Dover Publications, Inc.
31 East Second St.
Mineola, New York 11501

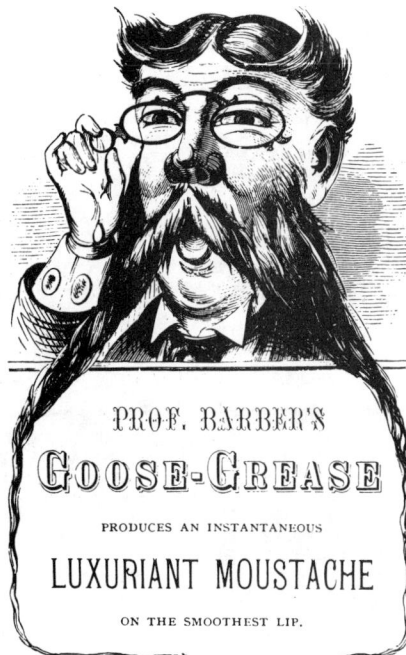

In addition to services like Dynamic Graphics and Dover Paperbound books, many book, office supply and art stores sell books of clip art for borders and illustrations. They also sell "press-on" or "rub-on" lettering sheets in a wide variety of typestyles.

Two companies that carry the whole range of graphic arts aids are Letraset USA Inc. and Formatt Graphic Products Corp. Their products vary in application and range of alphabets, borders and illustrations. Their catalogs contain easy-to-follow instructions on basic and creative uses of all their products.

Letraset
instant lettering

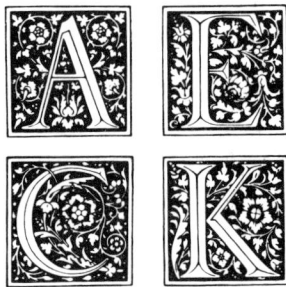

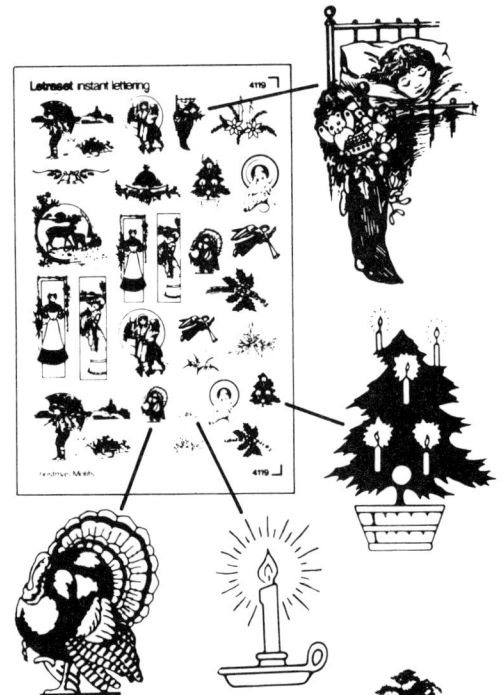

F☼RMATT

No. 6427

No. 6643   Other sizes styles on this sheet

LEADERSHIP IN THE CRE
DAYTIME — Page 52
LEADERSHIP IN THE CREATIO
DEEP — Page 52
LEADERSHIP IN THE CRE
DIMENSION — Page 52
LEADERSHIP IN TH
EUROSTILE BOLD SHADED — Page 52

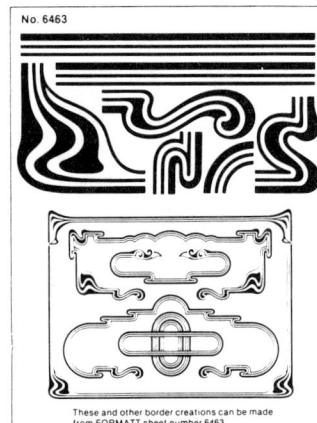

No. 6437

No. 6463

These and other border creations can be made from FORMATT sheet number 6463

Letraset instant lettering   4119

Christmas Motifs   4119

d. **Copy**

Review the basics of newspaper copy-writing covered in more detail back on page 92. Just remember to:

1. Use a prominent benefit headline.

2. Make your copy complete.

3. State the price or the range of prices.

4. Urge your readers to buy now.

5. Don't forget your store name and address.

6. Don't be too clever.

7. Don't use unusual or difficult words.

8. Don't generalize.

9. Don't make excessive claims.

10. KEEP IT SIMPLE, BE CONSISTENT and SELL!

While doing some consulting work for the National Retail Merchants Association, I had the opportunity to attend one of their advertising seminars in San Francisco. One of the speakers made a very descriptive point regarding the importance of strong selling copy in a newspaper ad. He took out a one dollar bill and held it in one hand and a one-hundred dollar bill and held it in the other hand. He said that both of these bills were the same size and compared them to two newspaper ads equal in size. It would cost you the same amount of money to run the "ad" in the right hand as it would the "ad" in the left hand. The difference is in the value of the messages contained in the ads. The stronger the copy, the more valuable the ad. Don't run a $1 message in a $100 space!

e. **For more information**

Write to the: Newspaper Advertising Bureau
4055 Wilshire Boulevard, Suite 529
Los Angeles, California 90013

Radio Advertising

Radio broadcasting had its official beginning in the United States in 1910 when Dr. Lee De Forest, the "father of radio broadcasting," transmitted a live performance direct from the stage of the world famous Metropolitan Opera House in New York City. His invention of the audion tube, in 1906, enabled wireless transmissions of electro-magnetic energy to carry the energy patterns of sound. Guglielmo Marconi, an Italian inventor, had discovered the secret of wireless communication even earlier and went on to build a global business in wireless telegraphy.

In 1919 and 1920, Pittsburgh's experimental station 8XK, owned by Dr. Frank Conrad, assistant Chief Engineer of the Westinghouse Electric and Manufacturing Company, scheduled regular music and talk programs. A local music store provided Conrad with records in exchange for announcements stating that the recordings were available at the Hamilton Music Store of Williamsburg. Although it was in a barter form, the Hamilton "mentions" on the air probably constituted the world's first radio advertising.

Today, radio has become a very selective medium that reaches different kinds of people through different kinds of programming. Radio allows you to target your advertising message to specific markets. . .young adults, Blacks, women, Hispanics, senior citizens, etc.

Basically, radio stations are divided into the following format categories:

1. Middle-of-the-road
2. Country
3. All Talk
4. Progressive Rock
5. Soft Rock
6. All News
7. Classical
8. Ethnic
9. Contemporary
10. Beautiful Music

All the local radio stations in your area should be considered on the basis of the kind of audience they deliver. . .the size of that audience compared to the cost, and whether or not that particular audience is the same as the description of your "average customer".

Advantages

Some of the advantages of radio as an ad medium are:

1. Flexibility.

   Ads can be placed and/or changed on relatively short notice. This allows you to take advantage of last minute sales or market conditions, i.e. "First snow of the year sale", etc.

2. Target marketing.

   Radio allows you to "rifle" in on a specific market since each station designs its format to appeal to a particular type of audience.

3. Intrusiveness.

   If your potential customers have their radios turned on at home or in the car, and if your commercial is designed to "catch their ear" they may hear your advertising whether they want to or not.

4. Reach and frequency.

   The definition of reach and frequency is how many people you reach and how often you reach them. Due to it's relatively low cost, radio gives you the ability to reach a wide segment of your target market over and over and over again. You can saturate your local area with your advertising message creating a sense of urgency on the part of your listening audience.

5. Urgency.

   My personal feeling is that radio is used most effectively to create an "act now" urgency. Many advertisers I have worked with have put together special three day sales or weekend sales and saturated the area with radio advertising for three days creating that "act now" urgency. The spots motivated the audience to take immediate action. . ."Hurry, don't miss out, sale ends tonight at 6 PM" or "The greatest sale ever to hit Fresno starts tomorrow morning at 9 AM. . .first come first served" or "Every item in our stock is on sale during our two day clearance sale. . .

savings up to 50%. . .hurry while the selection is good", etc. Remember, due to the audience listening in their cars, you have the ability to create some impulse sales by motivating a highly mobile audience to take action right now. They may just decide after listening to your "urgent message" to drive by and see what's going on.

Buying Radio Time

Radio stations, like newspapers and TV stations, base the price you pay for commercials on the size of the market, the number of people reached and the kind (age, income, family size, etc.) of people reached. But there is another factor that influences the price you'll pay for a radio or TV spot that doesn't apply to newspapers. That is the amount of inventory that is available when you're ready to buy. Let me explain. Newspapers never have an inventory problem. They can always meet the demand by simply expanding the size of the newspaper. Have you ever noticed how thick the newspaper is on Thanksgiving Day? Since the Friday after Thanksgiving is traditionally the biggest day of the year for the retailer, everybody wants to advertise their huge Thanksgiving sales in Thursday's paper. No problem. The newspaper just adds as many pages as necessary to be able to accommodate every advertiser. Nobody is turned away. There's plenty of room for everyone.

That's not the case in broadcasting. There are only 16 good, revenue-producing hours in the broadcast day and the National Association of Radio Boradcasters advises member radio stations not to exceed 18 minutes of advertising within any given hour. Many radio stations broadcast even fewer than 18 commercial minutes per hour. So, you can see why radio stations have an inventory problem during peak time periods. They've only got so many commercial minutes to sell and once they're gone. . . they're gone. More popular, higher rated stations find themselves in a "sold-out" position most of the time. When the demand consistently exceeds the supply. . .they raise their rates.

On the other side of the coin, many radio stations during certain times of the year find themselves with a lot of unsold time on their hands. Any broadcaster will tell you "radio and TV time is the most highly perishable commodity there is." If a radio station has a 60-second time slot open at 8

AM on Friday and it goes unsold. . .it's gone. . .it can't be sold tomorrow or the next day. That perishable inventory just went "poof" into thin air because it is "time" and time cannot be recaptured and sold again.

It's important for you to understand how perishable broadcast time is and how the law of supply and demand affects it's pricing. There may be certain times of the year when you're in a strong negotiating position. The stations may find they've got a lot of inventory going unsold. They may be willing to sell it below regular rates rather than not at all. However, there are other times of the year when you're lucky to be able to get on the air at any price.

Buy the summer, Thanksgiving, and Christmas periods well in advance and negotiate for better rates during the slow periods. Talk to your radio reps. Find out when the "sold out" and the "slow times" are in your market.

Radio Rates

When you look at a radio station's rate card, you will notice that it is divided into different time classifications. The time classification is based upon the amount of audience delivered and the rate that is charged for that particular time period.

While the following breakdown may vary from market to market, it will give you a general idea of how radio time is priced, from the most expensive area to the least expensive. But remember, this could even vary from station to station in your area:

1. **AM Drive Time — 6 AM-10 AM — Monday-Friday.**

This is the station's highest rated area since it delivers more people than any other time period. Stop and think how many people wake up to a clock radio, or turn on a radio to get the morning news and weather, or listen to the radio on their way to work and you can understand why this is "prime time" for a radio station.

2. PM Drive Time — 3 PM-7 PM — Monday-Friday.

This is a station's second highest rated listener area and reaches people as they're driving home from work or preparing dinner.

3. Daytime — 10 AM-3 PM — Monday-Friday.

This is considered excellent housewife time.

4. Weekend — 10 AM-7 PM — Saturday and Sunday.

You'll pick up a mobile audience that's usually on their way somewhere, involved in some form of leisure activity, or working around the house. This time period is especially good during the summer in many markets.

5. Evening — 7 PM-12 Midnight — Monday-Sunday.

Depending upon the station and it's programming format, this can be an excellent time period to reach teenagers.

6. Overnight — 12 Midnight-6 AM — Monday-Sunday.

Some talk show hosts have a very loyal and responsive "night owl" audience which can be reached during this period for very little money.

7. Sunday AM — 6 AM-10 AM — Sunday.

Many Stations carry religious programming, public service programming, or weekly news programs during this time period.

While it's possible for you to buy just "drive times" or only "weekends", etc., most stations make available special "package plans" where you receive a combination of announcements usually covering all time periods at a special package price. Work closely with your media reps. They can advise you on the best way to buy their station. With an enthusiastic and conscientious rep working for you, you'll have fewer problems and get better rates.

Sample Radio Rate Card

Please note: Rates vary from market to market depending upon the size of the market. These rates are used merely an an example and may or may not be representative of the cost of radio time in your area.

TIME CLASSIFICATION		SECTION I 1X	SECTION I 12X	SECTION I 18X	SECTION I 24X	SECTION II 12X	SECTION II 18X	SECTION II 24X	SECTION III 12X	SECTION III 18X	SECTION III 24X	SECTION IV 12X	SECTION IV 18X	SECTION IV 24X
AAA 5:30-10 AM M-F • 7:00-10 AM SAT	60 SEC	22.50	18.00	17.00	16.00	17.00	16.00	15.00	16.00	15.00	14.50	15.00	14.00	13.50
	30 SEC	18.00	14.40	13.50	12.50	13.50	12.50	12.00	13.00	12.00	11.50	12.00	11.00	10.50
AA 3:00-7:30 PM M-F	60 SEC	19.50	13.50	12.00	11.50	13.00	11.50	11.00	12.00	11.00	10.50	11.00	10.50	10.00
	30 SEC	15.50	10.50	10.00	9.50	10.50	9.50	9.00	10.00	9.00	8.50	9.50	8.50	8.00
A 10:00-3 PM M-F 10:00-7:30 PM SAT & SUN	60 SEC	12.50	10.00	9.50	9.00	9.50	9.00	8.50	9.00	8.00	7.50	8.50	7.50	7.00
	30 SEC	10.00	8.00	7.50	7.00	7.50	7.00	6.50	7.00	6.50	6.00	6.50	6.00	5.50
B 7:30-12AM M-SUN • 5-5:30AM M-SUN 5:30-7AM SAT • 6:00-10AM SUN	60 SEC	11.00	7.50	6.50	6.00	7.00	6.50	6.00	6.00	5.75	5.50	5.75	5.50	5.00
	30 SEC	9.00	7.00	5.50	5.00	5.50	5.00	4.50	5.00	4.50	4.25	4.50	4.25	4.00

WEEKLY TOTAL AUDIENCE PLANS		SECTION I	SECTION II	SECTION III	SECTION IV
12 TAP 3AAA 3AA 3A 3B	60 SEC	135.00	121.00	116.00	109.00
	30 SEC	110.00	100.00	95.00	88.00
18 TAP 4AAA 5AA 5A 4B	60 SEC	182.00	173.00	160.00	151.00
	30 SEC	147.00	137.00	129.00	120.00
24 TAP 6AAA 6AA 6A 6B	60 SEC	230.00	233.00	216.00	192.00
	30 SEC	184.00	173.00	163.00	161.00

For C Time Rates (Midnight to 5:00 AM) and Annual Frequency Rates, contact Station Representative. Subject to availability and clearance. ★ 120 days rate protection for continuing advertisers.

HELPFUL INFORMATION
...from the AD PLANNER

LOCAL RADIO STATION REVIEW

Station	Sales Rep	Phone #	Station Format	Profile of Avg. Listener	Rate Information
1.					
2.					
3.					
4.					
5.					
6.					
7.					
8.					

NOTE: Listen to each station and record your opinions. Start a file on each radio station containing rate cards and miscellaneous information. Use this form for quick reference.

CPM — Cost Per Thousand

Regardless of the time period or package you buy, the most important thing you want to know is, "How many people am I reaching for the dollars spent? What's my cost per thousand?"

You determine your CPM (cost per thousand) by using the following formula:

Ad Cost ÷ by
Number of thousands of   =   CPM (cost per thousand)
audience reached

For example, in a smaller market, if you paid $14 for a radio commercial that reached 7,000 adults 18 +, your CPM would be:

$$\frac{\$14}{7(000)} = \$2 \text{ cost per thousand for adults } 18+$$

In a larger market, you could pay $140 for a radio commercial but if you reached 70,000 adults 18 + you would also have a $2 CPM.

You should try to apply a CPM formula to every media buy you make, whether its newspaper, direct mail, radio or TV. If you have any questions, or you're not sure where to get the audience estimates to use, talk to your media rep and tell him you want a cost per thousand breakout on the schedule he's proposing.

But make sure you're comparing apples to apples. An enthusiastic media salesman can find "something" that they're "#1" in. . ."We're first in teens reached". . ."We're first in adults 40 + ". . .We're first in number of employees working for a radio station for two years or more", etc.

In figuring CPM's (cost per thousand) between radio stations, make sure it is a fair comparison based on the same criteria:

a. Use the same demographic group (adults 18 +, women 18-49 or whatever your target audience is) for all comparisons.

b. Compare coverage in the same geographic area whether it's ADI (area of dominant influence) metro area, county area, etc.

c. Compare information taken from the same rating source. For example, base your ratings comparison on the most recent Arbitron Radio Report or The Pulse or whatever recognized survey report is primarily used in your area.

Spend some time with the media reps and learn about the various rating services, how they work and their effect on the structuring of advertising rates. It's well worth your effort. It will save you thousands of dollars in wasted media buys if you can get to know and understand what a good CPM is and then apply that formula before you make any media buy. You'll quickly be able to see what's a good buy and what's overpriced. Remember, you're not buying a "spot" or an "ad". You're buying **"audience reached"** and unless you know how many people you're reaching and at what cost. . . you don't really know what you're buying! You just made a blind purchase. Maybe the buy will work for you and maybe it won't. But, you'll waste fewer advertising dollars if you buy **"measureable audiences"** rather than "air time" or "ad space". We'll discuss CPM's and rating services again in Section 4 when I talk about buying TV time.

"Would you ask Mr. Arbitron to step out into the hall for a minute please?"

Producing A Good Radio Spot

There are many avenues open to you:

1. Let the station do it.

Most radio stations are equipped to write and record your radio commercial, or it can be read live by the announcer on shift during the time period your commercial is scheduled. This is the most inexpensive way to "produce" your radio commercials. The only drawback to this approach is that your commercial may "blend in" with the regular programming of the station. There's nothing to make your commercial stand out. . .nothing to make people take notice and listen.

2. Produce a "broadcast logo".

Remember, when we were talking about your newspaper advertising, I said that you needed a logo and a distinctive border or layout to make your print advertising consistent, noticeable and distinctively yours! I feel the same is true for all of your broadcast advertising. You need a consistent sound, a consistent "broadcast logo" that makes all of your broadcast advertising distinctively yours. You accomplish this through the use of a musical image and/or distinctive voice on all of your commercials.

Let's talk about these two elements. First, the musical image or "jingle". There are a variety of ways for you to acquire your own musical image:

a. Buy one from a music production company.

There are many companies around that specialize in producing musical jingles for local and national advertisers. The Media General Broadcast Services, Inc. of Memphis, Tennessee, is probably the largest producer of custom and syndicated radio and TV jingles. The address is 2714 Union Ext., Memphis, Tennessee 38112, (901) 320-4375. They can produce an excellent musical image for local use for about $2400.

There are numerous other companies known for innovative arrangements and orchestrations. Tuesday Productions, Inc. is one of them at 11021 Via Frontera, San Diego, CA 92127 619-451-3333. My own company, Bay West Advertising, produces musical jingles for local and national clients, with prices starting at around $1800 for local use. We have some syndicated packages for less. The custom music you hear on our cassettes was produced by us especially for The Small Business Ad Planner.

Prices ranging from $1500 for a local-use-only jingle, to $25,000 plus for big production national-use jingles may make the national production houses too expensive for your limited budget. So, look at the next alternative.

b. See what's available locally.

Ask your media reps if they know of any local recording studios, musical groups or advertising agencies that are producing custom jingles for local clients. You may discover that you've got a talented producer of musical jingles in your own backyard who's willing to work with you and produce a custom musical arrangement for $1200 or less. (How far under may depend on how good a negotiator you are!) Be sure to tell them you want it to be a one time charge — *no residuals!* And you want a 60-second, 30-second and 10-second version with a 60-second and 30-second "instrumental only" version as well.

c. Contact your local college.

Call the music department at your local college. Tell them you are looking for a talented music student who could compose and produce a musical jingle for your business. You'll have five eager music students pounding on your door begging for an opportunity to compose a musical image. They'll welcome the opportunity to have something they've written actually "played on the air". If you make the right contact, he should be able to compose it, arrange it, find the musicians, record it and give you a finished product for under $750. You've got a custom musical image for a very low price and he may have a good start on a new career.

You'll have to explain to him exactly what you want. I recommend you produce a "donut" jingle. The following pages explain various types of musical formats.

116

d. Go to your radio station.

If you decide not to buy a jingle or produce one yourself, then go through the music library at your local radio station and look for "music cleared for commercial use." While this isn't as good as having your own custom jingle, it's the most inexpensive way (free!) to find a piece of music that fits your business. Select music that projects your company's personality, and appeals to your target audience. Be careful you don't allow your personal preference to overpower your customers' preference. For example, you may own a saddlery and your customers are all "country music" fans, but your personal music preference is "classical". Go with what your customers like.

Once you find just the right sound, have the radio station put it on tape for you. You can use that piece of music on all future commercials. Before long that music will become identifiable with you. It will become your musical image.

It's important the music you choose be "cleared for commercial use". Most stations subscribe to a production service which provides them with cleared music. You don't have to worry about paying residuals or violating any copyrights. The station has paid all the necessary fees and provides this as a service for the advertisers.

If you don't take advantage of the radio station's music service or create your own custom music, you're taking a chance of violating copyright laws when you decide that "Moon River" sounds just great on all of your commercials. You may like the idea, but Andy Williams, Henry Mancini, ASCAP and their attornies will not be too hot for the idea!

3. **Use of a distinctive voice and copy length.**

Radio is one human being talking to another human being. It is a "one-on-one" communication device. In order for your radio commercials to be most effective you want a voice that projects a warm, friendly, believable, enthusiastic image of your business. You want a distinctive voice that stands out from the rest of the commercials. For these reasons, I've always been opposed to the on-duty D.J. reading my client's copy live. Where does his weather forecast or chatter or another commercial end and yours begin? The only exception is if you use a personality with a loyal following, giving a personal endorsement of your product. I think Paul Harvey could tell his listeners to buy Confederate War Bonds and they'd start calling Southern post offices!

When you look for a spokesperson with a good voice to represent your business, he or she doesn't necessarily have to be a professional announcer. They just have to sound good and articulate well. You may be able to do your own commercials to add that personal touch. But be careful! Don't let your ego get in the way. It is logical and beneficial for some small business owners to do their own commercials. It is a disaster for others to attempt it. The important thing is that you find a voice and a musical sound that you can call your own, and then repeat it and repeat it. *Be Consistent!*

While 30's are bought on occasion, the standard length radio spot is 60 seconds. It's a better buy for the money. I've included a radio script form for you to use in writing your radio commercials. Note the number of words contained in a 30 second and a 60 second commercial. For more information on radio, write:

Radio Advertising Bureau, Inc.
485 Lexington Ave.
New York, New York 10017

"Hubert likes to play along with the musical jingles on TV and radio."

the small business AD PLANNER

RADIO SCRIPT

Company: _____

Title: _____

Length: _____ **Spot #:** _____

Co-op: _____ **Date:** _____

10 Second Spot = 25 Words   30 Second Spot = 75 Words   60 Second Spot = 150 Words

SECTION THREE REVIEW NOTES

Let's review what we talked about in the third section:

1. It's your advertising program and in order to structure and execute it successfully, you should attempt to know as much about your local media opportunities as you do about your own business.

2. Newspapers have been the number one advertising medium since colonial times due to their flexibility, production simplicity and ability to offer the advertiser measured results.

3. Newspapers, like all other media, base their rates on the number of people they reach. It is to your advantage to spend some time with your newspaper reps so they can thoroughly explain their rate cards to you.

4. Learn the essentials of an effective newspaper ad outlined on pages 91 to 94.

5. Regarding the production of your newspaper ads, you can let the newspaper produce them, hire a free-lance artist, hire an advertising agency or do them yourself.

6. Look into the various graphic art services available to you, such as Dynamic Graphics.

7. Some of the advantages of radio as an ad medium are: flexibility, target marketing, intrusiveness, reach and frequency, and urgency.

8. Learn how to buy radio time to best "rifle" your message at your target audience.

9. Effective radio commercials use a distinctive voice and/or strong musical image to attract and hold the listeners attention.

10. It's possible for you to produce your own "broadcast logo" once you learn how to structure the format for your jingle.

SECTION 4

"TELEVISION ADVERTISING"

Every time I conduct an advertising seminar, someone always asks the question "WHAT IS THE BEST FORM OF ADVERTISING?" My answer is immediate and given without hesitation..."The best form of advertising is the advertising that works best for you!"

I'm not trying to avoid the question. My point is that every business is different and each market area is different and budgets are different. You cannot make a blanket statement that says TV is better than radio, or radio is better than newspaper or newspaper is the best form of advertising. What works very well for one business may not be as good for another business.

In order for you to find out what will work best for you, you need to take the time to review the merits of every form of advertising. And even if you have a very small budget, don't automatically discount the possibility of TV advertising because you think it's too expensive. Television is a powerful salesperson and it deserves your review:

• 97% of the homes in the U.S. have television; 83% of these homes have color television; 50% have two or more sets.

• Americans spend more time watching TV than doing any other leisure time activity. 95% of all adults in America view some television in the course of a week.

• The average household spends over six hours in front of the TV every day.

• The average adult woman spends more than three hours a day watching TV.

The statistics, the surveys, the success stories, the facts are very impressive. There is no other medium that has the ability to reach as many people as fast as television! O.K. ...I made my point...there's no question, television has the ability to "reach people," but what about it's ability to motivate them to buy? Television is a powerful salesman. It's the next step up from one-on-one personal selling.

Television through the use of color, sound, motion and emotion literally reaches out and grabs your attention. You're locked in for thirty seconds to the message that's being presented, in a dramatic and colorful way. It's you and the TV commercial. . .one-on-one with no interruptions. You're a captive audience.

Fear!

O.K., if TV is such a powerful advertising salesman, then why don't more local retailers use it? That's easy. They're afraid of it!

1. They don't understand it and they haven't taken the time to learn about TV. So, they are afraid of what they do not know. It's much easier to produce and place an ad in the newspaper or on radio and just "forget" about TV.

2. They're afraid it will cost too much. . ."I can't afford TV!" I've heard that objection many times. In some cases it's a valid statement, but the majority of the time the local retailer simply has not done his homework and hasn't even explored the possibility of TV.

Let's take a look at the tube and see if we can overcome the "fear" of television advertising.

What Are You Buying?

When you purchase newspaper or magazine space or radio or TV time, you must understand what you're buying. You're not buying an "ad" or a "commercial". *You're buying the audience* that the "ad" or "commercial" is going to deliver! And remember this is measured by CPM's or the cost per thousand. You want your advertising to be "cost efficient". In other words, you want to reach as many potential customers as you can at the lowest possible cost. You want the lowest CPM possible. That's why "audience" figures are so important to TV.

Highly Competitive Business

If a program gets good ratings, it's being viewed by a large audience which means the network can demand more money from the advertisers because of the high audience delivery. If the ratings drop, the revenue drops, until finally the ratings drop so low the show is dropped and replaced with another show that will hopefully do better in the ratings. The A.C. Nielsen Company and Arbitron are the two most widely accepted television rating services. A portion of an Associated Press article for June 18, 1986 told the following story:

CANCELED SITCOM'S RATINGS REBOUND

NEW YORK (AP) — The Nielsen ratings have made NBC's programmers look like geniuses this year, but this week a show that the network canceled for next season turned up in the top five.

"All Is Forgiven" finished its nine-week run on NBC with the fourth-highest rating in the weekly A.C. Nielsen Co. survey, a robust 21.4 and a 34 percent share of the audience in its time slot.

Nonetheless, NBC spokesman Gene Walsh said in Los Angeles Tuesday, there is no chance of a reprieve for the sitcom, which stars Bess Armstrong as the producer of a daffy soap opera.

The ratings for "All Is Forgiven" may overestimate the program's strength for two reasons: it was up against reruns, and it had a strong lead-in on Thursday nights from "Cheers."

NBC won the weekly ratings chase last week, sweeping the top five and placing 17 programs in the top 30.

"Looks like the ratings are in."

"The Cosby Show" finished No. 1 with a 25.4 rating and 48 percent of the audience in its time period, followed by "Family Ties," "Cheers," "All Is Forgiven" and "Golden Girls," all on NBC.

Rounding out the top 10 were "Growing Pains," "2020" and "Who's the Boss?" all on ABC, and three shows tied for ninth: "227" on NBC, "Murder, She Wrote" on CBS and "Hardcastle & McCormick" on ABC.

Each rating point equals 859,000 homes with television. The share is the percentage of sets in use during the time period.

It's a highly competitive business and audiences are very fickle. A show that is popular today could turn into a "bomb" six months from now. People change and that's why programs change. The television industry strives to give the viewing public what they want. Ratings are the name of the game. . .no ratings, no audience. . .no audience, no advertisers. . .no advertisers, no money. . .no money, no show!

Local Ratings Battle

The same ratings battle that takes place on the national level also takes place on the local level.

Local TV stations receive most of their revenue selling advertising time in programs they originate locally. Examples of locally originated shows are syndicated programs which local TV stations buy from syndication companies, such as "I Love Lucy", "The Brady Bunch", "Happy Days", "Beverly Hillbillies", etc. Local stations also run movies and locally produced programs such as kid's shows, community interest shows, and the early and late news.

The biggest revenue producers are the early and late newscasts. They usually carry 8 minutes of advertising per half hour newscast. While the revenues are greater, the costs are greater, too. Top-rated news programs are produced by top-rated news staffs backed by the latest in equipment and technology.

In addition to producing revenue for the stations, the early news is also a very important lead-in to the "prime access" programming from 6:00 to 8:00 o'clock p.m. which is another good revenue producing time period.

How Much Does TV Time Cost?

There are two factors that determine the rate you should pay for TV advertising: Audience Size and Inventory Availability.

1. **Audience size.**

   TV stations price their rates according to audience size. Let's look at three thirty-second spots in a smaller market, say the size of Omaha, Nebraska, having three different rates and three different audience estimates.

   a. Today Show — 7-9 AM — cost $30

   b. Early News — 6-6:30 PM — cost $200

   c. Tonight Show — 11:30-12:30 PM — cost $35

   Now, if this was all the information you had, how could you determine if you were making a good buy? You couldn't! Unless you know how many viewers are watching each of these programs, you don't know what you're buying. If your target audience is total adults 18 years of age and older, then this is the added information you would need to determine if you were making a cost efficient buy:

   a. Today Show — 7-9 AM — $30 — adults 18+ = 8,000 viewers average.

      (Cost per thousand = ad cost ÷ the number of thousands of total audience)

      $$\frac{\$30}{8(000)} = \$3.75 \text{ CPM}$$

   b. Early News — 6-6:30 PM — $200 — adults 18+ = 34,000 viewers average.

      $$\frac{\$200}{34(000)} = \$5.88 \text{ CPM}$$

   c. Tonight Show — 11:30-12:30 PM — $35 — adults 18+ = 10,000 viewers average.

      $$\frac{\$35}{10(000)} = \$3.50 \text{ CPM}$$

   Please note that these rates are for example purposes only. Rates vary from market to market and these rates may or may not be representative of the average TV rates in your area. Consult your local TV rep for a detailed explanation of the cost of TV time in your market.

Naturally, news, prime time and 6 to 8 programs will be higher priced than daytime and late night programming due to limited inventory and they are "higher reach" programs. You pay more to reach more people at one time because they are different "unduplicated" people (those that you don't normally reach during another time period). But even with that thought in mind and based on the above calculations, tell your TV rep that you feel the CPM for adults 18 + for the news (5.88) is out of line compared to the CPM's for the Today Show (3.75) and Tonight Show (3.50). Therefore, you want to negotiate that early news rate down. You feel a more realistic rate would be around $140. That would give you a CPM of $140 ÷ 34(000) = $4.11 which is more in line with the rates established for the other programming you're buying.

Now you may not get the rate reduced from $200 to $140, because he'll probably tell you what I told you. . .news is a "higher reach" vehicle and therefore costs more. . .but it's worth a try. Be tough! Negotiate! Based on the above information, you've got a logical argument. Besides, **"negotiating"** a good media buy is half the fun of buying broadcast time.

When you ask your media reps to submit a cost per thousand proposal, make sure the audience estimates are taken from the same source — either the most recent Nielsen or Arbitron. The source should be noted so you know the information came from a legitimate rating service and not just "estimated" by a well meaning sales rep.

Nielsen and Arbitron provide very detailed audience estimate reports. The rating services refer to Metro Area, DMA (Designated Market Area), TSA (Total Survey Area) ADI (Area of Dominant Influence), ratings, share trends, four week averages, time period audiences quarter hour averages, total persons, total adults 18 +, men and women 18-34, 18-49, 25-49, 25-54, teen, children 2-11 and 6-11. In all, I think there are about 20 different age/sex categories.

You can (and most major agencies do) conduct all types of reach and frequency analysis and talk about GRP's (Gross Rating Points) and Cost Per Point and get so detailed you can give yourself a headache. So don't! KEEP IT SIMPLE! Don't frustrate yourself and make buying TV time more complicated than it needs to be. You don't have to become an expert at interpreting the ratings. As far as I'm concerned, all you need to know about the ratings are:

a. They are only estimates! They provide an intelligent basis for decision making and they're the best tools the industry has to work with, but they're not infallible.

b. How much will you be paying to reach your target audience? That is the group of people which most closely matches the customer profile you determined in Section 2. Your target audience may be all adults 18+, or women 18-49, or men 25-54, etc. When you have the audience estimates for your market, you can then calculate your CPM. If your advertising budget is large enough to warrant more sophisticated media analysis, I suggest you contact a good media buying service or advertising agency and let the professionals do it for you.

2. Inventory Availability

If audience size is the first consideration stations use to determine rates, the second factor is "inventory availability".

Television time, like radio time, is a highly perishable commodity. A television spot that is unsold at broadcast time loses 100 percent of it's value immediately. And that loss can never be recovered.

In addition to broadcast time being very perishable, it is also very limited. There are only so many spots for sale per day. A newspaper can add pages and accommodate everyone who wants to advertise. A TV station cannot add hours to the day. They only have so many spots to sell and once they're sold there are no more.

These two factors, high perishability and limited inventory, make TV time (and radio time) prime examples of the law of supply and demand. Some TV stations have a rate card that changes weekly based on inventory availability. Some TV stations work off of a "grid" rate card system. The fact is, rates change constantly and that's why you should negotiate the price when you buy TV time. Let me explain a grid rate card:

Spot Announcements — 30 seconds

Please note these rates are used for example purposes only and are not to be taken seriously.

	Level 1	2	3	4	5
Today Show, 7-9 AM	50	40	30	25	20
Morning Rotation, 9 AM-12:30 PM	60	50	40	30	25
Afternoon Rotation, 12:30-4:30 PM	60	50	40	30	25
Bonanza, 4:30-5:30 PM	70	60	50	40	30
Hollywood Squares, 5:30-6 PM	80	70	60	50	40
Early News, 6-7 PM	250	225	200	175	150
Etc.					

Now, based on this sample rate card for a smaller market, you could buy a 30-second commercial in the Today Show and pay anywhere from $20 to $50. If you try to buy the spot in December you will probably pay $50 due to the heavy Christmas business. If you wanted to buy it in January, you could probably get it for $20.

As a general rule, TV availabilities run like this:

January, February, March — slowest months, a lot of inventory available. Probably the best time to buy TV. There are a lot of people at home viewing TV and the rates are low. Your CPM's will never be better than during this period. Have some special sales and advertise on TV!

April, May, June — business is picking up, but there's still room for negotiating.

July, August, September — July and August are usually slow and a good time to negotiate. September is the beginning of the new fall season. Business starts picking up and rates start going up.

October, November, December — heaviest advertising months, limited avails (available inventory of commercials), higher rates. Buy early. Make your 4th quarter buys in January or February.

"If I Had Only Tried TV Sooner!"

If your business is located in a major market area like New York, Chicago, Los Angeles, etc., obviously TV time is going to deliver much higher audiences and will be priced accordingly. If you're a small business with a very limited budget, you may not be able to afford TV!

But, if you're located in a smaller or mid-size market such as Omaha, Des Moines, Fresno, Tuscon, Charlotte, etc., television may be the most cost efficient advertising buy you can make. At least it's worth looking into.

I know of some advertisers who wouldn't have anything to do with TV . . ."they simply couldn't afford it!" These same businessmen found themselves on hard times and were forced to close shop. Who did they call in order to advertise their final big "Going Out of Business Sale"? They called the TV salesman they wouldn't take the time to listen to before. They promoted their final sale on TV. . .had a phenomenal success. . .and were left wondering if things would have been different if only they had tried TV advertising sooner.

At Least Look Into It!

Analyze your market area, your budget, the cost of TV time and what you want to accomplish with your TV advertising. In my experience, television salesmen are very helpful. They will provide you with the information and guidance you need to plan a successful schedule.

Also keep in mind that you don't have to run a ton of TV spots to be effective. A small art gallery in Carmel, California, had a successful television advertising program on a very limited budget. They knew their target market was an older, better educated, more affluent adult. They analyzed that they could reach this target audience with 3-thirty second spots per week rotating in the Today Show from 7 to 9 AM.

Each month they shot six slides of the artist's work they were featuring and recorded the thirty second audio portion of the commercial on audio cassette in their office. The voice-over was done by the owner's wife who had a very distinctive accent.

The six slides and audio cassette were then delivered to the TV station by the 15th of the month. The TV station transferred the slides and audio cassette to video tape and the commercial for the following month was ready to go. They took a limited budget, but "rifled" in on their target audience and made every shot count. Obviously, TV worked for them. They were consistent TV advertisers even though they had a limited budget.

KEEP IT SIMPLE. . .BE CONSISTENT. . .AND SELL!

129

Buying TV Time

When you make your TV buys, keep the following points in mind:

1. Establish your target audience. Who do you want to reach? Adults 18 + ? Women 18-49? Teens?

2. Establish your TV budget. How much do you want to spend on TV?

3. Contact the Local Sales Manager at each of the TV stations in your area and ask him to have a salesman call on you.

4. Ask the salesman for a list of "avails' (available inventory for sale) that match your target audience. A spot in Lawrence Welk delivers more senior citizens. You'll reach teens with The Brady Bunch. The early and late news has a higher percentage of men, etc.

5. Ask for the "audience delivery" of each availability according to the latest ARB or Nielsen and to please calculate the CPM (cost per thousand) based on your target audience at the rates he quoted you. Make sure all the stations are working from the same rating book, i.e. The November ARB. Otherwise, you could be comparing apples with oranges!

6. Ask him about the production of your commercial. Can they help you write your commercial and produce it? Exactly what can they do and how much will it cost? (We'll talk about TV production next.)

7. Compare the various proposals. Look at the comparative CPM's. Negotiate the best buy. Buy as far in advance as possible at the lowest rates. Tell the sales rep that you've been offered a better package (if you have) by one of the other stations. Ask if he can better his original proposal. The better negotiator you are, the better the buy. Buy 30's. Unlike radio, rarely does the need justify the rate difference (60's are twice the cost of 30's) between a 60 second spot and a 30 second spot. 30's have become the standard of the TV industry.

8. After you're comfortable that everyone has submitted their best offer, make your decision. You may decide to "split" your buy between two or even three stations. Remember, you're buying audience. . .go with the best CPM's. People watch **TV programs,** they don't watch **TV stations.** There's little viewer loyalty to a particular TV station, only to TV

programs. You may find that station "XYZ" delivers the best CPM on their early and late news, but station "ZYX" delivers the best CPM in their early fringe times.

The only time you shouldn't consider splitting your buy is when one station makes you an offer you can't refuse, to get 100% of your TV buy. This kind of an offer can be done in a variety of ways...free production of your commercial, "bonus spots" (no-charge commercials over and above what you bought), exceptionally low rates on the time periods you want, etc. Listen to what everyone has to say and you be the judge. Either it's to your advantage to buy one station or more than one station.

9. Produce your commercials and get on the air. (Refer to the following production info.)

10. Measure your results. Analyze what you've done right or wrong.

"Well, it's about time!"

TV Production

If you're in a TV market that derives the majority of it's income from the local advertiser, your local TV stations have to be equipped to produce local commercials at a reasonable cost. Every local market I have worked in (and that was quite a few from coast-to-coast when I was handling Mr. Steak Advertising Co-ops) was blessed with one or more TV stations which could provide good production facilities for the local advertiser.

TV stations make their money selling TV time, not producing commercials. But in order to get you on the air they have to be equipped to produce your commercials. The less money you spend on producing commercials, the more money you have to spend on TV time.

Talk to your local TV reps. . .tour the stations. . .ask questions. Look at their production facilities. . .learn about TV production. . .view other commercials they have produced. Talk to their production director and tell him about your business and share some ideas you might have about your production. You'll find your visit to the TV studio an enjoyable and beneficial experience. This is the "fun" part of your advertising program. This is "show biz", so enjoy it!

Types of TV Production

Various stations are equipped to do different things. Some stations have the very latest state-of-the-art equipment and very knowledgeable production people. Others are not quite as good. However, they all have the production capabilities to produce a TV commercial for you.

Here are some possibilities with average costs, but please note that production costs will vary from station to station. Use these approximate costs per spot only as a guide. They could be high or they could be low depending on the size of the market you're in. Some stations may even be willing to produce your commercials at no charge to get you on the air.

1. **Slides/Voice-Over Announcer**

   This is probably the most inexpensive form of production, particularly if you shoot the slides and do the voice-over announcing yourself.

   The 35 mm slides can be shot at your place of business by you, or by the station's photographer or a photographer of your choosing. The station announcer can do the voice-over and add a little background music.

   When the station puts the slides and voice-over copy on to video tape they can dissolve from one slide to another in sync with the copy and if appropriate add some copy "supers" that say "Save 50%" or "Clearance Sale Now Going On", etc.

   Your last slide should be your logo slide giving your name and address in a fashion that is very easy to read. Hold on to it long enough to be read. . . at least 4 seconds. Approximate cost: Under $200.

2. **16 mm film transfer to video tape.**

   One step up from 35 mm slides is 16 mm film shot on location. Remember, you're dealing with a visual medium and the more action you have, the better your chances of catching and holding the audience's attention. Many local stations offer 16 mm sound-on-film shot on location. They edit the film and then transfer it to video tape in the studio adding any appropriate special effects and copy supers. While 16 mm film is still offered at some stations, it is rapidly being replaced by video tape in almost every market. Film cannot match the clear, sharp images of video tape. Approximate cost: Under $300.

3. **Video Tape commercial in the studio.**

   TV stations charge anywhere from $50 per hour to $300 per hour for "studio time". This means you can bring your props, merchandise, and talent to the studio and they will video tape your commercial using from one to three studio cameras and all the necessary lights, film chains, special effects, etc., necessary to achieve the desired commercial. If you are well prepared, know exactly what you want and have everything ready before you get in the studio. . .you can cut down your studio charges by getting in and getting out quickly and still create some very good commercials. Allow at least 2 hours per spot. Approximate cost: Under $400.

4. Mini-Cam on location.

The best equipped TV stations have mini-cam remote units that are equipped with a portable video tape TV camera and a ¾ inch or one inch video tape machine. These remote units have their own power source so they can go anywhere on location. . .the beach, the mountains, up a tree, etc., to produce commercials. The color quality, particularly on the one inch, is excellent. They've perfected the portable mini-cam units to the point that just about everything you can do with film you can now do with video tape. The big advantage with video tape is that you can play it back instantly and see what you just recorded. If you don't like the way it looks, you just do it again.

Normally, a two or tree man crew accompanies the remote unit and they will spend anywhere from an hour to a full day on location shooting the various scenes called for in the script. They then take the "raw footage" back to the studio where it is edited and "mixed" with the called for special effects, copy supers, and music to produce the finished commercial.

The advertiser pays for the remote (from $50 to $300 per hour) and then the time it takes to mix the spot in the studio (another $50 to $300 per hour) plus talent charges. Based on a four hour remote and a two hour mix with normal talent charges, your approximate cost will be: Under $600. (However, I know of instances where excellent mini-cam spots have been produced for as low as $200 — negotiate!)

Production Costs as % of Budget

Obviously, producing a TV commercial costs money. As a general rule of thumb, your production costs should not exceed 10% to 20% of your media budget. If you're going to spend $4000 on TV time, you shouldn't spend more than $800 on producing the commercials for that buy. If you can get **good** commercials produced for less, more power to you and the more money you'll have to spend on air time. But don't cut yourself short. Many advertisers hate to spend money on "production". They try to cut corners and as a result come out with a poor commercial that's not going to motivate anybody to do anything. By trying to save a little money on production they wasted every dime they spent on air time. You need a good selling commercial to produce good results. If it costs you a little money (within reason) to produce a **good commercial** . . .it's money well spent.

134

Produce A "Donut"

My advertising philosophy of KEEP IT SIMPLE. . .BE CONSISTENT. . . and SELL is very appropriate for producing TV commercials.

In order to get the most dollar mileage and most effectiveness from your TV spots, they should consistently present a positive image of your business. You can accomplish this by producing a commercial that has the same open and close, with a center section which can be changed to reflect seasonal sales or highlight different features of your business. This is called a "donut". Here's the way it looks.

```
(INTRO OPEN — APPROXIMATELY 10 SECONDS)
```

This part grabs the viewer's attention and provides the proper environment for you to sell your product.

```
(CENTER SELL — APPROXIMATELY 14 SECONDS)
```

This is the "hole" in the donut you can change as often as you like. You can produce a series of commercials. . .three, four or five different commercials. . .that have the same open and the same close, but different selling features in the center. You can feature various items and prices, departments, or sales, and you've got your TV commercials produced for the next six months at a reasonable cost.

```
(CLOSE — APPROXIMATELY 5 SECONDS)
```

This is where your logo and address appear, plus any identifying tag line you use, i.e., "So hurry to Barney's, your dollar stretching carpet dealer located on the corner of 5th and Charlotte."

Since you know you are going to be using the same open and close for quite some time, you can afford to produce a strong open and close.

The following is an example of some 30-second "donut" TV spots produced for two auto dealers in Santa Cruz. A total of three commercials were produced at the same production session. The open and close were the same on all three spots. The only difference was the center portion of the commercials. This approach to TV production has three advantages:

1. All of your commercials project the same CONSISTENT image.

2. You have the ability to change your "selling features" without having to produce an entirely new commercial.

3. You save on production costs. It's possible to produce "three" commercials for what it would normally cost you to do one.

TV SCRIPT

BAY WEST PRODUCTIONS

Client: SANTA CRUZ DODGE/DATSUN

Title: DUEL'N DEALERS — GENERAL, SPOT #1

Length: :30   **VTR #:** _____

Co-op: _____   **Date:** _____

Video	Audio
MCU Lee and Bob in western attire.	**(OPEN** - 12 seconds Musical Jingle)
Enter right to left, western street in background.	Jingle Up: Your Duel'n Dealers. . . .
Cut to: Low shot Lee and Bob, hands ready to draw, trigger fingers twitching.	
Cut to: Two shots of cowpokes #1 and #2 turning and reacting.	Santa Cruz Datsun. . . .
Cut to: CU of Bob's hand drawing and twirling gun.	
Cut to: Cowpoke #3 peering out from behind barn door.	Santa Cruz Dodge. . . .
Cut to: Lee's hand drawing and twirling gun.	
Cut to: Cowpoke #4 as mouth drops open in amazement.	
Cut to: Two shots Lee and Bob as they holster their guns and turn away to sit at desk in middle of car lot and greet customers rushing to get the best deal in town.	Your Duel'n Dealers are dealin' now. . .
Cut to: Long pan of car lot showing huge selection.	**(CENTER** - 13 seconds Lee on camera)
	Lee: We're out-deal'n every other dealer in town. We're writing unbelieveable deals on new Dodges and Datsuns. We've got the cars. . . We've got the financing and we've got the deals . . .Now is the time to buy!
Cut to: MCU Lee smiling as he blows imaginary smoke from tip of his gun and tips his hat with gun barrel.	**(CLOSE** - 4 seconds Musical Jingle)
Copy Super: Your Duelin' Dealers. . . Santa Cruz Dodge and Datsun 155 Center Street	Jingle Up: Your Duel'n Dealers are dealing now.
Fade Out	(Music Out)

137

Television Scripts

As you probably noticed from the Santa Cruz Dodge and Datsun spots, a television script is divided into the audio portion and the video portion. The audio portion consists of the copy to be read by the announcer, plus sound effects and/or music.

The video portion consists of a description of the visual action taking place while the copy is being read or music is being played. In order to produce a good TV commercial, it's important your TV script be easy to understand and your audio matches your video instructions. This can be accomplished by writing your commercial in either one of the following forms on the next two pages.

Normally, the dotted lines would not be on the first TV script. I put them in to show you how the video instructions need to correspond to the audio portion of the script. The more detailed your video instructions, the easier it will be for the director to interpret what you want and therefore produce a better commercial.

That's why many advertising agencies and TV stations use "storyboard scripts" to visually show what they want to take place in the commercial like the storyboard script that we did for Thompson's Water Seal.

I didn't reproduce the entire commercial, but I think you'll get the general idea. For your convenience, I've included some blank TV copy forms (one of each format) at the end of this section. You can make copies of them for use in writing your own TV commercials. If you want to use the storyboard script form, but can't draw, just use stick figures to convey the idea you're looking for.

TV SCRIPT FORM #1

Client: DIXON & SON TIRES

Title: TRUCK/TRACTOR/FLEET SERVICE

Length: :30   **VTR #:** 1

Co-op: _____   **Date:** _____

Video	Audio
Medium two shot of Harry and Dave at work.	(Music establish and under voice-over announcer.) Harry Dixon and his son Dave are very proud. . .
Cut to: Wide shot of retread operation as Harry walks into shot.	of their new tire service center in Watsonville, specializing in complete truck. . .tractor and fleet service. . .
Medium shot of Harry with service staff working in the background.	(Harry on camera speaking) "We offer the most modern truck retread operation in the Monterey Bay Area. . ."
Cut to: Medium close-up of Bandag operation. Copy Super: "Bandag Tread Rubber"	using only the toughest Bandag tread rubber
Cut to: Harry as he walks behind display of tires. Copy Super: "Harry Dixon" (signature)	at Dixon and Son Tire Company, you'll find dependable service at fair prices and I personally stand behind the work we do."
Cut to: Wide shot exterior of service center Copy Super: (logo and addresses)	(announcer) Dixon and Son Tire Company. . . now with two locations in Scotts Valley and Watsonville. (music up and out)

STORYBOARD SCRIPT FORM #2

Client: E.A. THOMPSON CO.

Title: THOMPSON WATER SEAL

Length: :30   VTR #: 012-EAT-2-30

Co-op: Date:

Video Instruction	Visual Representation	Audio
1 **Oceana Theatre** MWS pan of Pat Turley walking in front of performing seals. One seal is balancing a can of Thompson's Water Seal on his nose. VF: Pat Turley Senior Trainer Zoom into:		(Music up and under voice of Pat Turley:) "Here at Marine World/Africa USA, we have a lot of performing seals."
2 **Oceana Theatre** MS Pat as he stops next to seal balancing can. The seal tosses can to him and he holds it up. Wipe to center to:		"And one of our best performers is Thompson's Water Seal."
3 **Backstage** CU can of Thompson's Water Seal and reverse zoom to maintenance man spraying steps with seals playing in background.		"Thompson's is hard at work behind the scenes protecting against moisture damage." . . . etc., etc.

The Essentials of Good TV Production

1. Keep It Simple!

Don't try to say too much. You've only got 30 seconds so pick out one or two strong selling points and do a good job of getting those points across. If you try to do too much, your spot becomes confusing and you won't communicate any sales message to the viewer.

2. Be Consistent!

The competition is tough enough without competing with yourself. Don't change your advertising approach every other month. Adopt the image and style that fits your business and stick with it. Don't be "Barney the Dollar Stretchin', Money Savin' Carpet Dealer" one month and "Barnard's - the High Quality Carpet Store" the next month.

3. Sell!

The purpose of advertising is to sell! Don't be so clever and creative with your TV advertising that you forget to sell your product. You should have one goal with all of your advertising. . .Sell, Sell, Sell!

4. TV is a visual medium.

Remember to use both sight and sound on your TV commercials. That's what you're paying for, so take advantage of it. Use strong visuals to **show** your story. Use visual copy supers to **tell** your story. The test of a good TV spot is to turn the sound off and see if the visuals are strong enough to carry the sales message without the audio. Use good catchy music. . .strong visuals. . .an unusual voice to produce a spot that reaches out and grabs the viewer's attention.

5. Match the video with the audio.

Don't be saying one thing and showing another. Match your visuals with your audio or you'll confuse people.

6. Talent is where you find it.

The majority of the TV spots I've produced over the last 15 years have featured amateurs. . .people who had never been in a TV commercial before. (I'm proud to say that some of those people have gone on to become professionals.) Don't be afraid to ask your next door neighbor, your butcher, or one of your employees or relatives to be in your TV commercials. If they're really special, they could possibly even be an on-camera spokesperson for you. This is a one-on-one medium and if a person is sincere, has a nice appearance and sounds good in person. . . chances are they'll come across the same way on TV.

Have the Production Director assist you in your talent search. . .hold auditions. . .you might want to make a contest out of it.

At one time, in many of the smaller markets, there were only three or four "professional announcers" doing all the local commercials. You would see the same person doing four different commercials in a row for four different companies. Obviously, after a while that particular spokesperson started to lose credibility.

Don't feel you have to use a so-called "professional" to do your TV commercials. Look around. Talent is where you find it.

7. **Listen to the Production Director.**

Listen to the recommendations of the Production Director. His job is producing good TV commercials. That's what you're paying him to do, so let him do it.

8. **Enjoy yourself.**

This is the "fun" part of advertising. The more relaxed you are, the more relaxed the talent and crew is going to be and the better your commercials will turn out. This is "show biz" so relax, have fun and enjoy yourself.

"He thinks he's found the trouble. The picture tube is clogged with dead Indians."

STORYBOARD SCRIPT

Client: _____

Title: _____

Length: _____ **VTR #:** _____

Co-op: _____ **Date:** _____

Video Instruction	Visual Representation	Audio

SECTION FOUR REVIEW NOTES

Let's review what we talked about in the fourth section:

1. Television is a powerful salesman. Take the time to learn about it.

2. When you purchase print space or broadcast time, **you are buying the audience** your print ad or broadcast commercial is going to deliver.

3. TV rates are based on audience estimates. In order to know if you're getting a good buy, you have to know how many people you're reaching and calculate your cost per thousand.

4. January, February and March are the best months to buy TV time. You can negotiate an excellent buy due to the amount of inventory available.

5. Buy October, November and December early since these are normally heavy months and the available inventory of spot announcements is limited.

6. It's possible for you to buy TV with a limited budget by targeting your TV message to one segment of the market and consistently running your commercials within a certain area. For example, running three TV spots per week within the late news rotating Monday through Sunday.

7. Visit your local TV stations and talk to their production directors so you can learn the production possibilities available to you.

8. Follow the essentials of good TV production outlined on pages 141 and 142.

SECTION 5

"DIRECT MAIL, PR, YELLOW PAGES, PREMIUMS, FLYERS, AND MORE"

Direct Mail

Of the 13 billion pounds of mail delivered each year, over one-half of it is advertising material. But many small businesses have avoided the use of direct mail as an effective advertising medium because they believe "it's too expensive"!

Granted, the CPM (cost per thousand) is high with direct mail but I feel the higher cost is offset by direct mail's ability to target your advertising message to a select group of people. You may be reaching fewer people, but if done right, the people you are reaching are qualified potential buyers. The possibility of direct mail is worth exploring. There may be a place in your advertising budget for some direct mail programs.

What are the advantages of direct mail?

1. **It's highly selective.**

   You can target your message directly to your potential customer. If your primary trade area encompasses a three mile radius around your store, you can do a mailing that takes in just that area. If you own a children's clothing store and you're having a sale on toddlers clothes, you can obtain a mailing list of families in your area who have children one to three years of age. If you created a good system for accumulating the names of your customers and you want to have a private "customers only" sale, you've got a built-in way of reaching those customers through direct mail.

145

2. **It provides a captive audience.**

Once your direct mail recipient opens the direct mail piece. . .you've got a captive audience, at least for the moment.

3. **It's personal.**

You can speak directly to your potential customer and provide him with all the information and all the motivational reasons he needs to make a decision and take action.

Target Audience

Following my "KEEP IT SIMPLE" philosophy, I maintain all retailers are dealing with two groups of people:

1. Current Customers
2. Potential Customers

And your advertising has two objectives:

1. Encourage repeat business and higher Average Customer Transactions from current customers.
2. Turn potential customers into regular customers.

With this in mind, you need to determine if direct mail can be of benefit to you in dealing with current or potential customers.

1. **Current customers**

   a. Mailing list

   Remember, in the first section, I talked about Radio Shack and what a great job they did in compiling information on their customers and acquiring mailing lists for their catalog mailings by writing the name and address on the sales slip of **every purchase.** If you have the time, (obviously, a fast food restaurant can't take the time to ask and record the name of every customer) this is a great way to acquire a customer mailing list. When you have your sales slips printed, leave room for a name and address and just make this a normal part of every sale. Record the names in alphabetical order each evening, or at the end of a week or month onto a master list.

If your business doesn't allow the time on each transaction to obtain this information, hold a monthly drawing and give away some kind of prize valuable enough to encourage people to enter your drawing. Provide entry blanks, pencils and a deposit box in a high traffic location to motivate as many of your customers to enter as possible. While this won't provide you with a complete list of your customers, it will provide a good base from which to work.

It's not important how you acquire your list. . .through sales slips, contests, guest registration books, birthday clubs, customer comment cards, etc. . .**what's important is that you do acquire a customer list!** These names are very valuable and are a good source of potential increased revenue for your business.

b. Direct mail offer

Now that you have a list of current customers, what are you going to do with it? I recommend you experiment with different ideas until you hit the plan that works best for you. You could start by having a "Private Sale for Special Customers" on a once a year basis. This sale could be a one day, one week, or a one month event. Special invitations can be sent to your current customers containing discount coupons or special offers "not being offered to the general public". This also provides you with the opportunity to thank them for their past patronage and tell them how you're looking forward to serving them in the future.

If you get good response to this "Private Sale for Special Customers" event, you may want to do it quarterly.

c. Cost efficiency

Make sure your direct mail efforts are a profitable way to bring in new business. Keep accurate records and evaluate the cost efficiency of the event. As a general rule of thumb, the overall campaign budget should not exceed 5 to 10% of the amount of the new business gained. Before you hold your "special event" determine how much it is going to cost you. Include all postage costs (save money on the postage by using the Bulk Rate instead of First Class. It will save you money and won't hurt the effectiveness of your mailing), printing, any increased labor related to the event, cost of any free premium offers, etc. Then determine how much new business you need to generate to break even. Is that a realistic expectation? If not. . .rework the figures and see where you can cut costs and still have a valid promotion.

2. Non-customers

There is a big difference in a mailing going to a friend (customer) and one going to a stranger (non-customer).

Even if you're not successful in converting all of your customer mailings to direct sales, you at least derive some PR benefit from the mailing by letting your customers know they're appreciated. A customer mailing is a "no-risk" mailing. It will probably get read and it will do you some measure of good.

A non-customer mailing is a different story. It's more difficult to get a "stranger" to even open your direct mail piece and harder still to get them to respond to it. It's a "high risk" mailing, because you could get very little response from it and it could have been a very costly mistake,

If you are going to get involved in direct mail advertising beyond your current customer list mailings, then I suggest you take time to research what makes a direct mail program successful. Your need to consult an expert is in direct proportion to the amount of money you intend to spend. The more you spend, the more qualified advice you should solicit. You may think it looks easy, but it's not.

Here are the basics:

a. Clearly define your objective.

What is the purpose of your direct mail advertising? What do you hope to accomplish with it? Do you want to sell 50 washers and dryers on a "Special Purchase Private Sale"? Do you want to motivate 100 **new** customers to visit your store during the month of July to redeem "special gift" cards? Be as specific as possible with your objectives. Don't use direct mail as a "general" advertising medium. It's too expensive for that. It must SELL for you. Give it a specific job to do, targeted at a specific audience.

b. "Rifle" your message.

Reaching the right person at the right time always has been, and always will be, a prime key to advertising success. Direct mail definitely gives you the ability to "rifle" your advertising message at a specific target audience. Take full advantage of that ability. With a little research there's no reason why you can't obtain the right mailing list for your specific objectives and target audience. Mailing lists have become so sophisticated, it's possible to obtain one as broad as "every residence in your immediate zip code area" to as specific as "every doctor earning $100,000 + who drives an old Corvair, has 6 children, vacations in Northern Ireland, and owns property near Mount St. Helens!" (If you did acquire such a list, I wonder what you would be trying to sell him? INSURANCE!)

The age of computers has brought tremendous capabilities to the direct mail list industry. If you have ever purchased anything by direct mail, or subscribed to a magazine, or obtained a credit card, your name went on a mailing list that has been sold over and over again at the average price of $50 per thousand names. The industry has become so sophisticated that you can purchase the names of every five year old child who has joined the A & W Root Beer Birthday Club nation-wide! How about the 59,200 names on the Military Academy Alumni list or the list for the 3,840 Pawnbrokers in the U.S. or the 170 Macaroni and Spagetti Manufacturers.

If you would like information on exactly what lists are available, go to your local library and look through the "SRDS (Standard Rate and Data Service) Direct Mail Lists." If you haven't seen this publication before, you're going to be amazed. It's the size of the Chicago phone book and it lists lists!

Some people object to "their name being sold." However, the Presidential Commission on Privacy has reviewed the direct mail list industry very carefully. They have come to the conclusion there is no harm done by the rental of mailing lists to others. However, they did suggest people should have the right to have their name removed if they so desire.

c. List customer benefits.

Direct mail is no different than any other form of advertising. Your copy has to list "customer benefits". John Q. Public wants to know, "What's in it for me?" 50 to 60% of your offer should concentrate on the benefits of your offer. People aren't really interested in a glowing description of your product or your business. They want to know what value it has for them. Look at your offer from the customers point of view. . .think. . .Benefits. . .Benefits. . .Benefits!

• Promise a benefit in the headline or first paragraph.

• Enlarge upon that benefit.

• Back-up your offer with proofs and endorsements.

• Encourage the need to "act now".

d. Make the layout and copy fit the market.

When you talk to your target market, use language and illustrations they understand.

Your copy and layout approach would be different for college professors than for rodeo cowboys. You'd take one approach for teenagers, a totally different approach for senior citizens. Making your copy and layout fit the target audience and the offer can make the difference between success and failure. Keep it consistent with your print ads for reinforced recognition. Remember, recognition is cumulative!

e. Make it easy to take action.

You have made a specific offer to a specific target audience and you have listed specific customer benefits. Now. . .what do you want the customers to do? Call, visit, redeem a coupon, mail a pre-paid, pre-addressed reply card? Ask for the sale in such a way that it's easy for the customer to take action. KEEP IT SIMPLE.

- "Call 555-4567 and reserve your hand carved Wooden Indian today."
- "Visit Carl's Carpet Store anytime during the next 10 days and receive your FREE THROW RUG."
- "Just check box 1, 2 or 3 on the pre-addressed, pre-paid reply card and drop it in the mail today."

f. Don't quit too soon.

Many retailers have tried direct mail once, didn't get dramatic results, and quit. Research your direct mail programs. Analyze what you did right and what you did wrong. Review your copy, your offer, your mailing list. Maybe the timing was bad. . .maybe the offer wasn't strong enough. Don't quit too soon. With a few adjustments, you may have a tremendous winner. I believe you should give every advertising program you try a fair opportunity to prove itself to be a winner or a loser. If it was a good enough idea to even get involved with, then it deserves a fair test.

I heard a story (it's not a true story, but it makes a point) about a man who had a formula for a new soft drink called "4-Up", but it just wasn't quite right, so he added another ingredient and called it "5-Up". Still it wasn't right. He added a sixth ingredient. It didn't work and he quit.

Someone else picked up where he left off and added a seventh ingredient and the rest is history. In any endeavor you undertake, be it advertising, business or personal, never stop at "6-Up"!

Coupons. . .Coupons. . .Coupons

Their are numerous direct mail companies that specialize in coupon mailers. They will approach ten or twenty businesses and solicit a coupon offer from each one, print the coupons and mail the package to certain predetermined zip codes guaranteeing a 25,000, 50,000 or more distribution. The cost is usually very low and since the direct mail company does all the work (layout, typesetting, printing and mailing). It requires very little effort on the part of the small business owner. If your business lends itself to couponing, i.e., a pizza parlor, carpet cleaning service, ice cream parlor, car wash, camera store, etc., this is a very inexpensive way to distribute your coupons.

If one of these companies is not currently serving your area, you might want to explore putting together this kind of package yourself. Get nine of your business neighbors to participate and divide the costs among the 10 of you. Or you might want to approach the rest of the group with the idea that since you're putting the whole package together, you shouldn't have to pay anything. Naturally, it will require some effort on your part, but you'll receive a "Free Mailing" for your services.

If you decide to participate in a direct mail coupon distribution program similar to the one I described, make sure that you:

1. Make an offer on your coupon that is strong enough to motivate people to redeem it. In today's competitive market place, merely saying "present this coupon for 10% off" is not strong enough.

2. Understand the total costs involved in the program. Does layout and typesetting cost extra? Are there any "hidden charges"?

3. Know exactly when the coupon package will be delivered, where it will be delivered and how many will be delivered.

4. Be prepared to measure the results in a meaningful manner. How many coupons were redeemed, when were they redeemed and what was the total sales transaction attributed to the redemption of that coupon. You need to accurately measure the results of your direct mail couponing effort in order to determine if it's worth repeating.

Definition of Mail Order

I have been talking about using "direct mail" as a method of advertising to increase sales of current customers and reach new customers. There are two other terms "mail order" and "direct marketing" that people tend to use interchangeably with "direct mail". This can cause confusion because "direct mail", "mail order" and "direct marketing" really describe three different concepts:

Direct Mail is an advertising method, a means of bringing a business' services and products to the attention of potential customers. Catalogs and sales literature, a form of direct mail advertising, may be sent out by retail stores, wholesale outlets and other businesses as well as mail order firms.

Mail Order is a marketing technique, a way of doing business. Mail order companies have no direct contact with consumers, but solicit all orders through the mails or other advertising media. Buyers send orders and payments through the mail. Merchandise may be shipped by any suitable transportation mode. Some concerns operate only mail order functions; others conduct mail order departments as a sideline or special department.

Direct Marketing is a broad marketing concept that encompasses merchandising by mail. The industry defines it as a marketing system that offers products and services using various promotional media (including direct mail) in order to prompt a direct action response by mail, telephone, or personal visit. Any type of business can use direct marketing methods. A TV record offer which asks the viewer to telephone or mail an order is considered direct marketing; home product coupons mailed to the customer or printed in a newspaper and refundable at any food store is another example of direct marketing.

If you intend to get more involved in direct mail, mail order or direct marketing than the simple mailings I've been talking about, I suggest you attend some seminars, send for more information, and consult the experts in the business.

There are many companies which hold one day seminars around the country on direct mail/marketing. I've attended a number of these seminars and found them very informative. They provide a valuable education, stimulate your creative juices, and motivate you to take positive action. The best way to obtain a listing of seminars and general information on direct mail advertising is to subscribe to DM News. It's the newspaper of direct marketing and is distributed free of charge to qualified direct marketers and their agencies in North America. Audit and postal regulations require a written request from the subscriber. This written request must contain the following information: individual's name, job title, name and address of business, and nature of business. All inquiries should be signed and dated. Free subscriptions must be renewed each year. The cost of a subscription sent outside North America or to non-qualified subscribers is $24. per year, payable in advance. All inquiries regarding subscriptions should be mailed to:

Circulation Director
DM News
19 West 21st Street
New York, NY 10010.

I also suggest you order the booklet "Mail Order Enterprises", Vol. 11, No. 7, price $1, available from:

Small Business Reporter
The Bank of America
Department 3120
P.O. Box 37000
San Francisco, CA 94137

So far, the prices for obtaining information have been pretty good, right?. . . ."Free and $1"! But if you are really going to get serious about direct mail, then contact the main resource for information:

Direct Mail/Marketing Association, Inc.
6 East 43 Street
New York, New York 10017
(212) 689-4977

The DMMA is **the** professional international trade association of the direct mail/marketing business with offices in New York, Washington and Paris. It is the only trade association that fully covers direct marketing. They'll send you all kinds of valuable information including recommendations on some books to read.

There is also quite a few direct mail newsletters published that contain information on the newest developments in direct mail advertising. One such newsletter is called "Direct Respone, the Digest of Direct Marketing". It's published by Infomat, Inc., a company that specializes in direct response advertising and mailing list consultation. You can write for a free sample issue of their newsletter:

Direct Response
P.O. Box 2100
Rolling Hills Estates, CA 90274

Yellow Pages

Yellow Page advertising is an absolute necessity for some businesses and totally unnecessary for others. Only you can judge the importance

Yellow Page advertising will play in your advertising mix. Here are some questions and suggestions you can use to determine **your** need for Yellow Page advertising:

1. Are your customers already pre-sold on calling or visiting you and just using the yellow pages as a convenience to get your telephone number or address?

2. Or do the people in need of your kind of products or service, consult the Yellow Pages to see "what's available" and then make a decision to call or visit based on the effectiveness of the advertising?

3. How do your competitors handle their Yellow Page advertising?

4. Have you been running Yellow Page advertising over the past few years? What kind of response have you received? How much of your business can you directly trace to your Yellow Page advertising? Have you conducted a simple research project to measure it's effectiveness?

The Positive Side

The Bell System Yellow Page Advertising Department claims that an advertisement in the Yellow Pages gives you these advantages:

1. Circulation — The Yellow Pages are delivered to every telephone subscriber — home, business, office, factory and public telephone booth.

2. Usage — 85% of the Western adult population consult the Yellow Pages at one time or another for buying information.

3. Always Available — Yellow Page information is always available when needed 24 hours a day, every day of the year.

4. Follow-Up Action — 93% of all Yellow Page references are followed by a visit, phone call or a letter.

The Negative Side

The critics of Yellow Page advertising claim that it suffers from incomplete market coverage, clutter and infrequent usage as shown on the following page.

1. Circulation — Currently 2,300 local Yellow Page directories are published in the U.S. ranging in size from 3 to 4 pages to two-volume 2,500-page editions. Market coverage is incomplete with the smaller books and clutter is a major problem with the larger editions.

2. Usage — Studies show that 25% of adults 18+ use the Yellow Pages less than once a month and 17% never use Yellow Page directories.

How often do you use the Yellow Pages at work or anywhere else?	Percent of Adults 18+	
Never	16.6%	
Less than once per month	24.8%	
1-3 times per month	28.9%	83.4%
1-3 times per week	23.3%	
Once a day or more	6.4%	

I always find it interesting how sales people can say the same thing only say it a different way depending upon which side they're on. If you'll take a close look at the statistics above, you'll notice they're supposed to influence you **against** Yellow Page advertising. If you add up the last four statistics you'll discover that according to this particular study 83.4% of adults 18+ use the Yellow Pages at one time or another. The Bell System Yellow Pages Advertising Department uses basically the same statistics - 85% of the Western adult population consult the Yellow Pages at one time or another for buying information to influence you **in favor of** Yellow Page advertising.

O.K.! So much for influential statistics! My personal feeling is you have to judge if Yellow Page advertising is absolutely necessary for your particular kind of business and if it is, what's the minimum size ad you can run without losing out to your competition. KEEP IT SIMPLE. Don't go overboard in the Yellow Pages. It can be expensive and once you're locked into the monthly cost, there's no cancelling for at least a year.

I conducted an advertising seminar at Lake Tahoe, Nevada, for the American Building Contractors Association and had one of the home remodelers in attendance tell the group about a full page color ad he was running in the Los Angeles Yellow Pages. It had been out for four months and he said "I can't trace one single lead to that ad and what makes me sick is that I still have 8 months to go on my contract at $2,000 per month!!!!"

Magazine Advertising

Very few small businesses have even considered magazine advertising. Your first impression is one of "that's too rich for my blood." Maybe, but don't rule it out totally until you at least look into it.

Look at magazine advertising on these two levels:

1. **Local**

   There could be a variety of local magazine publications in your area.

   a. Chamber of Commerce publications

      Some of the local Chambers publish excellent magazines with a strong following of the local business community. If your target audience is local businessmen, this is a publication you should check out.

   b. Tourist publications

      If you're located in a "tourist town" and the tourist business is important to you, I'm sure you're already familar with your local tourist magazines.

   c. Entertainment magazines

      Some areas have local entertainment magazines distributed in hotels, motels and restaurants.

2. **National/Regional**

   Thanks to the marvels of computers today, almost one in five magazine ads is purchased in regional or demographic editions. As a result, it may be possible for you to buy Newsweek, Time, Sports Illustrated, etc., on a regional basis at a cost much lower than you would imagine. I know of one small business owner who bought one ad on a regional basis in Time Magazine and then merchandised that one ad in all of his other advertising, including POP. He had the ad laminated, made counter cards out of it and placed them on the counters of his jewelry store. He milked that one ad for 5 years worth of POP value. You've got to admit that seeing the tag line "as advertised in Time" is impressive for any advertiser.

If you have any questions regarding magazine advertising and you can't find the answer locally, contact the

Magazine Publisher's Association
575 Lexington Avenue
New York, New York 10022
(212) 752-0055

They're very helpful and will be more than happy to answer your questions or point you in the right direction.

Transit and Billboard Advertising

Transit and billboard advertising are good "visual reminders" to increase awareness of products already well-known or pre-sold. That's why you'll see many national advertisers using this form of advertising such as Folger's Coffee, Wrigley's Gum, Budweiser, Coca-Cola, etc.

Transit advertising (bus advertising) is available in about 400 markets. It is often called the "urban medium."

Since most of the billboards have been removed from the nation's highways, billboard advertising can be considered to be an urban medium also.

As you are well aware by now, I firmly believe the primary purpose of advertising is to SELL. By their very nature, transit and billboard advertising are limited in their sales ability. That's why they are used as "visual reminders" of products that are already well-known or pre-sold. **YOU** have to SELL! You're not well-known or pre-sold. Therefore, I don't think you can afford the luxury of transit or billboard advertising.

There are exceptions to this. I've had small business owners share their billboard success stories in my seminars. I had one gentleman remind me of the value of a billboard when it is strategically located in such a fashion that it can serve as a directional sign guiding people to your business. The billboard is still not "selling", but it is "directing" people how to get there, thus providing a valuable sales function.

When I was in Orlando, Florida, conducting a seminar for the National Tire Dealers and Retreaders Association, I was amazed at the number of billboards all over Florida. In an area that caters to the tourist trade, billboard advertising can be used very effectively to reach all those highly mobile visitors.

So there are exceptions, but as a general rule, I will stand behind my original statement.

Premiums, Incentives and Advertising Specialties

Premiums and incentives are products that are used to motivate people to take some kind of action. . .buy your product, do a better job, save more money, come back more often, try a new product, redeem a coupon, order early, work more hours, etc. What's the difference between a premium and an incentive? Glad you asked! It just so happens that Bill Anderson, editor of *Potentials in Marketing* and an expert in the industry, has the answer:

"In recent years, the term 'incentive' has been gaining in popularity to describe products used to motivate. In truth there is no difference between a 'premium' and an 'incentive,' except that a premium is simply the product itself, nothing else. An incentive, however, carries with it the concept of motivation towards action. Thus you might promote the 'incentive' for a sales or consumer program; while after the event you would ship them their 'premium.'

In practice 'premiums' and 'incentives' are pretty much the same; products used to motivate by reward. The term 'premium' is usually used in conjunction with programs used to motivate the consumer. . . consumer premiums. . .and the term 'incentive' is usually used in conjunction with programs used to motivate salespeople, dealers, etc. . . .sales incentives."

O.K., that clarifies the difference between a premium and an incentive, so where do advertising specialty items fit in? An advertising specialty item is inexpensive and designed specifically as a carrier of an advertising message. It is usually distributed free of charge as a goodwill gesture on your part and as a means to make people more aware of your business.

As a general rule, when you are trying to motivate a **consumer** to take some action you will use a premium item or an advertising specialty item. For example:

"Open a new savings account in the amount of $300 or more at First Boston Bank and receive a Free Teddy Bear!"

- the teddy bear would be the premium item and the cost of the teddy bears to First Boston would be absorbed in the overall cost of running the promotion.

"Boys and girls come see Ronald McDonald in person this weekend at the McDonald's in Galesburg and receive a FREE Ronald McDonald coloring book".

- the Ronald McDonald coloring book would be an advertising specialty item used for PR and motivational purposes.

When you are trying to motivate your **employees** to work harder or sell more, you would use a sales incentive item:

"Every salesperson who sells twenty of our special Christmas candles this week will receive dinner for two at Andre's."

- dinner for two becomes a strong motivational incentive to sell Christmas candles.

"They're handing these out free, sir, over at the Gigantic Food Mart opening!"

Don't buy t-shirts, balloons, calendars, pens or coffee mugs because you like to see your name in print. Don't let your ego get in the way. Buy premium sales incentives and/or advertising specialties because you have a logical plan in mind on how to use them to help increase sales:

- plan your premium promotions

- pick the right items for the right market

- purchase wisely, don't overbuy

- and shop around for the best price.

Premium items can be a valuable motivational tool in your overall advertising and sales program if you use them properly.

If you don't use sound business judgement in your purchase of premium items, you could end up with 1,000-1983 calendars in your back room as Dick Clark welcomes in 1984 from Times Square!

"Sure, you got a good buy — but what are we going to do with 640,000 1976 calendars?"

For more information on this area of advertising, write to the premium related trade associations:

National Premium Sales Executives, Inc.
1600 Route 22
Union, New Jersey 07083

Incentive Manufacturers and Representatives Association
7912 Ardleigh Street
Philadelphia, Pennsylvania 19118

Promotion Marketing Association of America, Inc.
322 8th Avenue, Suite 1201
New York, New York 1001

Specialty Advertising Association International
1404 Walnut Hill Lane
Irving, Texas 75038

Community Relations and Public Relations

I believe Community Relations efforts and Public Relations activities are two different things.

1. Here are some examples of what I classify as "Community Relations efforts":
   - Sponsoring a Little League baseball team or soccer team.
   - Running an ad in your daughter's high school yearbook.
   - Contributing a gift certificate to the local school carnival.
   - Sponsoring a bowling team.
   - Running an ad in the monthly Rotary newsletter, etc.

From a results-obtained versus dollars-spent standpoint, these are not efficient ways to advertise. They're not "selling" forms of advertising. In fact, any advertising benefit derived is secondary. The truth of the matter is, you're making a donation. And that's O.K. I feel every business owner should be community minded and support worthwhile projects within reason. But, don't kid yourself. Go into these efforts knowing that you're making a donation. . .and not advertising.

For your own protection, so these Community Relations contributions don't get out of hand, establish a separate Community Relations budget and stick to it. Once the money is earmarked. . .just tell the next high school yearbook salesman or team sponsor solicitor your budget is allocated for the year, but you will consider them in next year's allocations.

You really have to be careful about "a small ad here. . .a small ad there . . .a gift certificate here. . .a donation there, etc." Before you know it, all of these $10 or $20 expenditures "shotgunned" all over the place have added up to thousands of dollars.

2. Here are some examples of Public Relations activities:

   • Obtaining a story in your local newspaper about the rare 1800's coin collection you have on display.

   • Obtaining print and broadcast exposure for you and your business as chairman of your local United Way campaign.

   • Obtaining print and broadcast publicity for the local boy scout troop that's going to build "the world's largest ice cream sundae", in your parking lot.

Public Relations activities are any efforts on your part to obtain **free media publicity** while attempting to promote a positive image in the minds of the public for you or your business. Many local publications are looking for interesting and worthwhile stories and would be happy to give you some "free publicity" if you can provide them with a good story. In order to do that you need to:

a. Get in the habit of thinking **"possible PR story"** and looking for stories about you or your business that would be of interest to the general public. This is not always easy. You need an interesting angle that will capture the editor's and the public's imaginations. . .

   • "Local Grocery Store Owner by Day. . .Volunteer Policeman by Night"

   • "The Pins Really Add Up. . .CPA Bowls His Second 300 Game"

   • "Three Generations of Browns Have Been Serving Hamburgers at The Hamburger House"

   • "Local Retailer Writes the President. . .and Receives a Reply"

   • "Pulling Taffy for a Living"

b. Whenever you think you've got an idea for a "possible PR story" -**write it down!** You don't have to worry about it being a literary work of art. Even if it's in outline form, just get it down on paper. 98% of the great ideas and stories are lost because people simply don't take the time to write them down. If you don't use it right away, you can keep it in a file to use later.

c. Start a file on "PR stories" clipped from your area newspapers and magazines. Note the subject matter. What kinds of stories are being published? Who wrote the story?

d. Develop key media contacts. Review your "PR stories" file, and note the names of the writers who are writing the majority of the human interest stories. When you're ready to submit your story idea for publication, call that writer and tell her (or him) you've read many of her stories and how much you have enjoyed them. Tell her you have an idea for an interesting story and you want to see if you can schedule an appointment to share it with her.

An effective PR program is worth the effort to generate valuable exposure "that money can't buy."

Hand-Out Flyers

Many small businesses have colorful one-sheet advertising flyers printed to advertise a sale, or a special discount, or just to communicate general advertising information. Is this form of advertising beneficial? I would say "yes, if you have a logical way to distribute your flyers," but only you can measure its cost efficiency for your particular business.

If you want to try advertising flyers, keep the following points in mind:

1. **Production**

You want your advertising flyer to be attractive, while spending as little money as possible producing it. You can accomplish this by designing a basic format consisting of your logo and a distinctive border. (Just as I recommended for your newspaper advertising.)

Have two layouts measuring 5½ x 8½ each on one standard size sheet of paper, so you can get two flyers from each 8½ x 11 sheet of paper. By doing it this way, you can have 250-8½ x 11 copies run; cut them in half; and come out with 500-5½ x 8½ advertising flyers. You get twice as many flyers for the same amount of money.

Keep the original border artwork to use each time you want to run flyers. Just change the body copy containing the special offer.

To save costs, hand letter or type the body copy of the flyer and have it printed at the least expensive quick printing place you can find. You should be able to obtain 500 flyers for under $15.

2. **Distribution**

The key to a successful advertising flyer program is good distribution. Your 500 flyers will do you absolutely no good sitting in your back room, in the trunk of your son's car, or in the bottom drawer of your friend's desk at the neighborhood service station.

Research the distribution possibilities in your neighborhood:

- Can you work a trade with other merchants. . .you'll distribute their flyers if they'll distribute yours?

- Are there any upcoming parades, carnivals, special events, etc., that will draw large crowds of people?

- Are there any shoppers' information booths in your area?

The most attractive flyers containing "the greatest 50% off discount sale ever offered" are useless if you can't establish an effective way to distribute them.

On a Saturday afternoon in May, my wife and I took our two young daughters to the San Jose Civic Auditorium to see "Sesame Street Live". Just outside the entrance to the auditorium, a teenage boy handed us a flyer with the headline "Save 33% on the Best in Family Entertainment." The 8½ x 11 flyer promoted some upcoming family entertainment shows like "The Pickle Family Circus", "Little Red Riding Hood" and "A Christmas Dream" and encouraged us to order tickets early to save as much as 33% off the regular price. What a good example of target marketing! Isn't it logical to assume that everyone going to see "Sesame Street Live" would also be potential buyers of tickets for other family entertainment events? And do you know a better way to reach those people than to stand in front of the auditorium and hand them an inexpensive flyer as they're walking in?

One other point on distribution. Nothing will alienate your neighbors more than to have their parking lots or yards littered with your advertising flyers. Be careful how you hand out your flyers so they're not scattered to the four winds. It's a good idea to print the following in small print on the bottom of every flyer:

> "We sincerely hope you'll redeem this valuable coupon at (name of shop or restaurant). However, if you can't, please dispose of it in a proper receptacle. Thank you for not littering!

3. Measuring Results

Your first impression regarding the cost of this kind of advertising is "only $15 for 500 flyers, that's cheap!" But, is it? Look at your CPM (cost per thousand). Assuming all 500 flyers were distributed to 500 adults, and not counting your labor costs for distributing the flyers, your CPM would be:

$$\frac{\$15}{.5(00)} \quad = \quad \$30 \text{ CPM}$$

Thirty dollars per one thousand advertising impressions is not a good CPM unless you get very strong response from your efforts.

In order to judge if advertising flyers are worth your effort, you need to:

a. Have a strong coupon offer on your flyer. Buy one, get one free; 40% off; free gift for visiting your store; etc. The offer has to be strong enough to motivate a customer to walk in the door carrying the flyer coupon offer.

b. Measure your response. Keep track of every flyer coupon redeemed by writing the date and the amount of the sale on the back. At the end of the promotion add up the total amount of sales generated. Measure these figures against the cost of printing and distributing the flyers to see if this was a successful form of advertising.

Business Brochures

Many businesses (amusement parks, hotels, motels, insurance brokers, etc.) find it an absolute necessity to have an attractive brochure available telling about their business or facility. Whenever they receive an inquiry, they simply mail a brochure. Whenever they make a sales call, they leave a brochure as a summary of their sales effort.

Obviously, an expensive four-color sales brochure complete with photos, illustrations and glowing copy is not practical for the majority of small retail operations.

However, it is nice for every business to have some kind of printed sales piece briefly describing the business, for distribution to potential customers.

You should take advantage of every opportunity to invite people to visit your shop or restaurant. You don't have to go to the expense of a four-color brochure, but you should have **some kind** of printed sales piece telling who you are, what you have to sell and where you're located.

KEEP IT SIMPLE. If you don't need an elaborate brochure just have some oversized business cards printed containing sales information. Or combine the advantages of a business card, a premium item and a brochure all into one hand-out piece. Design it as a business card/brochure for you with a "reminder of his and her sizes", "frequently called telephone numbers", or a "list of area recreation facilities", etc., for your customer.

I produced an advertising campaign for Mr. E.A. Thompson of Thompson's Water Seal involving a tie-in with Marine World/Africa U.S.A. As a result, I got to know Mr. Thompson and discovered what an enthusiastic salesman he is. He carries wallet size calendars promoting Thompson's Water Seal with him everywhere he goes and passes them out generously. I know right now there are cab drivers, bell boys, waiters, hotel managers and restaurant owners all over the world carrying a Thompson's Water Seal calendar thanks to Mr. Thompson. He never passed up any opportunity to say hello and sell Thompson's Water Seal. We should all be as enthusiastic about our business as he is about his.

Printing

We've been talking about having advertising flyers, brochures and/or business cards printed. I'd like to make a few comments about working with printers. The first thing you need to realize is that there is a big difference between a quick printer, a medium-size printer and a large printer.

1. A Quick Printer

If you need a simple flyer printed in a hurry at an inexpensive price, a small quick-print operation is just what you're looking for. A quick printer is in business to do exactly what his name implys, print a lot of small jobs in a short period of time at a low price. Simple print jobs should be taken to a quick printer. You'll find them to be efficient at what they do best.

2. A Medium-Size Printer

A medium-size printer picks up where the quick printer leaves off. They're usually equipped to set type, do layout and pasteup and handle larger quantity runs. They're a little more sophisticated in what they have to offer you in the variety and quality of paper stocks, inks, typesetting and graphic design. While a quick printer specializes in smaller runs of "camera-ready" printing that you deliver to them, a medium-size printer is usually a little better equipped to get involved in the printing process at the beginning of the job. The medium-size printer can do the typesetting, layout and pasteup to make your job "camera ready" for them to print.

3. A Large Printer

The bigger the job, the larger the printer you'll need. If you want 50,000 four-color brochures featuring seven different photos in an eight-fold format, you'll need to find a printer large enough and sophisticated enough to handle your job. The larger printers have salesmen that come to you and they're accustomed to dealing in large quantities and very high quality work.

Choose a printer that best fits your needs. Don't take a quick-print job to a medium or large-size printer. The good ones won't accept your business and will advise you to take it to a smaller printer anyway. On the other hand, don't ask any printer to do a job that's beyond his capabilities. He may try to stretch to get the business and you could both end up being very unhappy. Learn the capabilities and the limitations of the printers you deal with and use the right printer for the right job.

When you decide to use a particular printer, make sure:

1. The printer fully understands exactly what you want and is confident he can deliver the job the way you want it when you want it.

2. You fully understand what the finished product is going to look like and agree with it.

3. You know how much you will be charged before the work is started. Ask for a breakdown of the charges so you can see exactly how much you paid for the typesetting or layout or paper stock, etc.

4. You understand everything involved in the printing of your job:
   - layout
   - typesetting
   - pasteup
   - paper stock selection
   - ink colors
   - folding
   - colating
   - number of halftones
   - color separations
   - etc., etc.

If you can learn what a printer can and cannot do, you'll be in a much better position to save yourself money and achieve higher quality printing.

"You there! How soon can you get out a proclamation?"

Bus Benches, Sandwich Boards and Restroom Advertising

Small business owners seem to fall pray to "gimmick" advertising salesmen. I think the reason is many small businesses have the mistaken notion that they can't afford the normal forms of mass media advertising. . . radio, TV and newspaper. . . .so they turn to alternative "less expensive" forms of gimmick advertising. The problem with this thinking is very seldom do the alternative forms of advertising work. So, instead of being "less expensive" they end up being **very expensive.**

I had a client come to me one time and say he was approached by a salesman who had a revolutionary advertising idea. The salesman wanted him to buy space on his "restroom advertising board". This man was trying to put a "network of restrooms" together. His idea was to take two foot by two foot boards, fill them with ads, laminate them, and then hang them above all the urinals in area gas stations and restaurants. He said he could guarantee a 50 urinal circulation with a minimum of 500 exposures per day to a captive audience!!!!!

Over the years I have seen far too many small businesses take respectable advertising budgets and try a little of this and a little of that. . .an ad here. . .an ad there and literally "shotgun" their advertising budget all over the place. As a result, they received poor results and wasted thousands of dollars. They also lost the benefit of the increased sales an effective advertising program that "rifled" in on their target customer could have brought them.

As a general rule, stay away from the numerous gimmick forms of advertising. Save your advertising dollars to use in the proven forms of advertising where they'll do you the most good. . .TV, radio, newspaper, direct mail. You don't have any dollars to waste, so "rifle-in" with your advertising buys and avoid the "shotgun" approach.

SECTION FIVE REVIEW NOTES

Let's review what we talked about in the fifth section:

1. The advantages of direct mail advertising are: it's selective, provides a captive audience and it's personal.

2. Your direct mail approach should take into consideration whether or not you're dealing with current customers or potential customers.

3. As a general rule, there's room in your marketing mix for at least one "current customer" mailing per year and possibly more.

4. Yellow Page advertising is an absolute necessity for some businesses and unnecessary for others. Only you can judge its importance to you.

5. Review magazine advertising on two levels: local and national. It's possible to buy national magazines on a regional basis at a much lower cost.

6. Transit and billboard advertising are good "visual reminders" to increase awareness of products already well-known or pre-sold.

7. There are many different ways to use premium items in your business. Just don't go overboard and end up with 1500 out-of-date calendars in your back room.

8. Learn the difference between community relations and public relations and then set a definite budget for these areas and stick to it.

9. Hand-out flyers are only effective if you have a logical system for distributing them and you monitor the results.

10. It's possible to turn a simple business card into a "business brochure" so you have some kind of printed sales piece to distribute at every opportunity.

11. Avoid the numerous forms of "gimmick advertising". Save your advertising dollars for the basics — radio, TV and newspaper. You don't have any dollars to waste so "rifle-in" with your advertising buys and avoid the "shotgun" approach.

12. Learn how to best work with your local printers in order to obtain the highest quality work at the lowest possible cost.

"It's our gimmick advertising doll - you wind it up and it doesn't work!"

SECTION 6

"YOUR ADVERTISING PLAN, AD AGENCIES AND RESULTS"

Your Advertising Plan

O.K., if you've done your homework, you should now be ready to start structuring your Annual Advertising Plan. Let's review and make sure you've gathered all the tools necessary to build your plan:

1. You have your house in order.

2. You have your employees well-trained.

3. You know who you are and what you have to offer.

4. You know who your customers are.

5. You established an advertising budget.

6. You translated the above information into an appropriate creative format that fits the personality of your business and appeals to your target customer.

7. You have reviewed the various advertising media possibilities available to you.

Objectives, Strategies and Recommendations

You need to take three elements into consideration in structuring your advertising plan:

1. **Your objective**
What do you want to accomplish?

173

2. **Your strategy**

How are you going to attain your objective?

3. **Your specific recommendations**

What are the specific details and the specific actions required to carry out your strategy?

In order to better understand this planning process, consider this simple example:

You haven't eaten all day and you're hungry.

1. Your objective — "to satisfy your hunger."

Now you have a lot of options open to you. . .you can eat at home, eat at a restaurant, or have a snack at your desk. Whatever you choose becomes your **strategy** for accomplishing the **objective** of satisfying your hunger. Let's say you decide to eat out, then. . .

2. Your strategy — "to eat at a restaurant."

But which restaurant? French, Chinese, Bar-B-Q? How will you get to the restaurant? Who will go with you? What will you order? How much will it cost? Will they accept credit cards? Which ones? You need to deal with all of the above specific recommendations in order to carry out your **strategy** of eating at a restaurant to accomplish your **objective** of satisfying your hunger. Therefore. . .

3. Your specific recommendations —

- I'll eat at Joe's Bar-B-Q.
- I'll drive my car.
- My wife and daughter will accompany me.
- I'll order bar-b-q'd ribs, cole slaw, french fries and ice tea.
- I'll pay cash for the meal.

Details, Details, Details

The first two elements of the advertising plan are relatively easy to put together.

1. Your objective(s) —

Be as specific as possible, don't just say "to increase sales", say "to increase sales by 25% or "to increase gross sales by an average of $2000 per week."

You could have multiple objectives.
a. Increase sales by 25%
b. Increase average customer transactions (A.C.T.) by $5 per transaction.
c. Change your image in the eyes of the consumer from a "discount house" to a "quality operation."
d. Increase the average visits of your current customers from once per month to twice per month.

2. Your strategy —

If you used multiple objectives, you need a corresponding strategy for each objective. Following the list of objectives above, your corresponding strategies would be:
a. Allocate an estimated advertising budget of $12,000 based on a 2% of sales figure.
b. Institute an employee incentive program called "A.C.T. Now" to motivate our sales people to increase their average customer transactions.
c. Hire a free-lance artist to produce a new logo, newspaper format, POP materials and sketch ideas for a new layout of the store's interior aimed at projecting a higher quality image.
d. Create a bounce-back coupon program designed to increase the number of visits of current customers.

3. Your specific recommendations —

Now we get to the dollars and cents part. You have to take all the bits and pieces of information you've been gathering and organize them into a specific Annual Advertising Plan containing as many details as humanly possible aimed at executing each of the above strategies. Budget how much you are going to spend every month and what you're going to spend it on.

I recommend you start with the step-by-step process used in the following sample form to first determine how much of your advertising budget needs to be reserved for "advertising support services" and how much can be allocated to purchasing media advertising.

HELPFUL INFORMATION ...from the AD PLANNER

ADVERTISING BUDGET ANALYSIS

For Carl's Carpet Store

Use this sample form to determine how much of your advertising budget can be used to purchase media advertising.

	Cost	%	Budget	%
A. Determine your annual budget			$12,000	100%
B. Subtract the fixed advertising costs you're "locked into"				
• Merchants' association co-op $100 per month	1,200	10		
• Yellow Pages $50 a month	600	5		
Subtotal of fixed costs	− 1,800	15%		
C. Subtract the dollars budgeted for various internal advertising expenditures				
• POP signs and displays	500	4.2		
• Employee incentive programs	400	3.3		
• Bounce-back coupons/flyers	200	1.6		
Subtotal of internal costs	− 1,100	9.1%		
D. Subtract the dollars budgeted for various PR or community relations projects				
• Rotary Club ads	120	1		
• Daughter's yearbook ad	100	.8		
• Sponsorship of bowling team	240	2		
• Reserve for additional PR	200	1.6		
Subtotal of PR budget	− 660	5.4%		
E. Subtract the dollars you have budgeted for various production costs				
• Artist fees for finished art for print and POP layouts	600	5		
• Production costs for producing 6 radio and 3 TV spots	1,200	10		
Subtotal of production costs	− 1,800	15%	− 5,360	− 44.5%
Subtotal = Budget Remaining For Media Buys			= $ 6,640	55.5%

How Are The Dollars Being Spent?

Based on the example analysis, note that only 55.5% of the budget is going towards media buys aimed at motivating new customers to visit Carl's Carpet Store. 44.5% of the budget is committed to internal programs, PR and production costs. Review your overall budget to make sure you're getting the maximum efficiency out of every dollar you're spending. I recommend at least 60% of your budget, higher if possible, should be used to buy media advertising — radio, TV, newspaper, direct mail, etc., in order to generate increased sales.

The important thing is to identify where the dollars are going. Separate your budget into the example categories so you can see exactly how much you're actually spending on:

1. **Reaching and motivating new customers.**

   a. Radio, TV, newspaper, direct mail efforts.

   b. All other budget expenditures having an objective of reaching people, selling them and motivating them to visit your business.

   This is the positive **"working"** part of your advertising budget and should be **where the majority of your budget is spent.** Remember, the purpose of advertising is to SELL!

2. **Advertising support services.**

   a. Production budgets to produce your radio, TV and newspaper ads or direct mail programs.

   b. PR or community relations budget you feel obligated to or sincerely want to do.

   c. Internal POP and displays, employee incentives, etc.

   d. Advertising specialties, i.e., matches, t-shirts, buttons, etc.

This is the "back-up" portion of your budget. These expenditures may be necessary, but they don't, by themselves, ring the cash register. They help you **get ready,** or provide the proper internal environment for the **"working"** part of your advertising budget to be more effective.

As I mentioned earlier, at least 60% or more of your budget should go toward reaching and motivating new customers. It's difficult to "sell" new people on coming to your shop or restaurant if you don't have any advertising salesmen (radio spots, TV spots, newspaper ads, etc.) out on the street. In order to sell people your product or service. . .you have to reach and motivate people. To reach and motivate people, you have to spend your advertising dollars where they'll do you the most good.

"It's Not Working" and For Good Reason!

I had a client approach me a few years back and complain business was bad and his advertising just wasn't working. He couldn't understand it. After all, he was spending $25,000 a year on advertising and he just couldn't see where it was helping him.

"I think you're working too hard on that Ad Budget Analysis, Ralph."

After analyzing his budget, I discovered he was very active in the community and was a member of a lot of service and trade organizations. He supported just about every high school play, PTA carnival and Little League function held during the year. He was an "easy touch" for every charitable organization in town and he charged every donation, trade show trip and luncheon expense against his advertising budget.

His $25,000 advertising budget looked like this:

A. Total budget $25,000

B. Fixed advertising costs
- Yellow Pages, merchants' association, trade shows, club dues, lunches and dinners $ 4,000

C. Internal Advertising Expenditures
- POP signs, displays, employee incentives, window painting $ 1,000

D. PR and Community Relations
- High school ads, carnival ads, contributions to numerous civic organizations $ 8,000

E. Production Costs

Free-lance artist on retainer, production creative service on retainer, miscellaneous production expenses $ 3,000

Subtotal of "Support Services" — 64% — $16,000

Amount Left for Media Buys — 36% — $ 9,000

No wonder his advertising wasn't working! He was only spending $9,000 on reaching and motivating new customers to his business! $16,000 was being spent on charities, community relations and production related advertising expenditures. How did he expect his advertising to work if he didn't have any advertising salesmen. . .radio, TV, newspaper ads. . .out on the streets selling? The first step toward solving his advertising problem was to reallocate the budget. He needed to reverse his percentages and spend 64% ($16,000) on media purchases and 36% ($9,000) on "back-up" support services.

Structuring The Media Plan

Let's assume my client reversed his budget percentages and ended up with $16,000 for media buys. How should he allocate his media expenditures for the year? What's his advertising plan?

Media planning is the process of designing a course of action that shows how advertising time and space will be used to help accomplish your marketing objectives.

There are many different approaches to structuring your media plan depending upon the type of business you're in, your budget, your local market conditions, your sales curve, etc. I would like to share three possibilities with you.

1. **Method A — Consistent Monthly Expenditures**

   With this approach, your budget and media buys are fairly consistent every month of the year. If your monthly sales are equal throughout the year and your business requires more "consistent awareness" than "promotional pushes", you may want to divide your budget by 12 (using our example $16,000 ÷ 12 = $1333 per month) and make your media buys based on this amount each month.

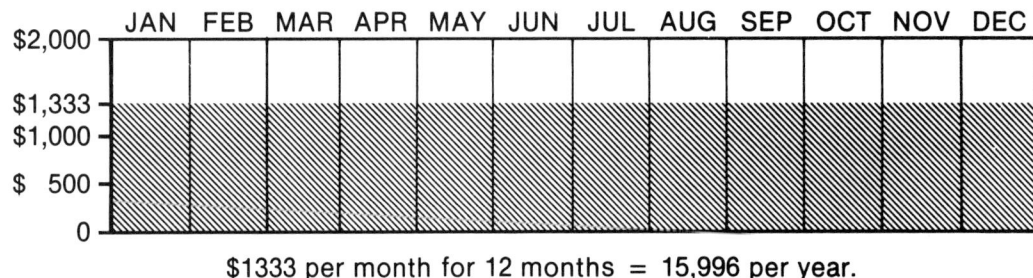

$1333 per month for 12 months = 15,996 per year.

   If "equal monthly media expenditures" make sense for you, then after you determine how much you have to spend each month, decide how you will spend it, i.e.

4 - quarter page newspaper ads per month at $250 each	=	$1000
1 - week of radio, 18 spots per week on 3rd week of each month	=	$ 340
		$1340

180

Now that you have decided to run four quarter-page newspaper ads and 18 radio spots per month, you can make your media buys and plan the production of your ads and radio spots well in advance.

2. Method B — Four Big Promotions

This method calls for you to divide your budget into four, or five, or six, or eight, etc., strategically placed promotions during the year. You concentrate all your efforts and budget on making these promotional efforts as hard-hitting and successful as possible. This concept is based on the premise that the competition for your customer's attention is fierce. Therefore, in order to make an impact, you have to hit the buying public hard enough and often enough, within a short period of time, to make them notice and take action. You grab the public's attention with a hard-hitting sale for three or four weeks and then lay off until your next promotion. Just as they're starting to forget about you, you're back on the air and in the newspapers again with another hard-hitting promotion. Place your promotions when you need them. . .when they will do your particular business the most good.

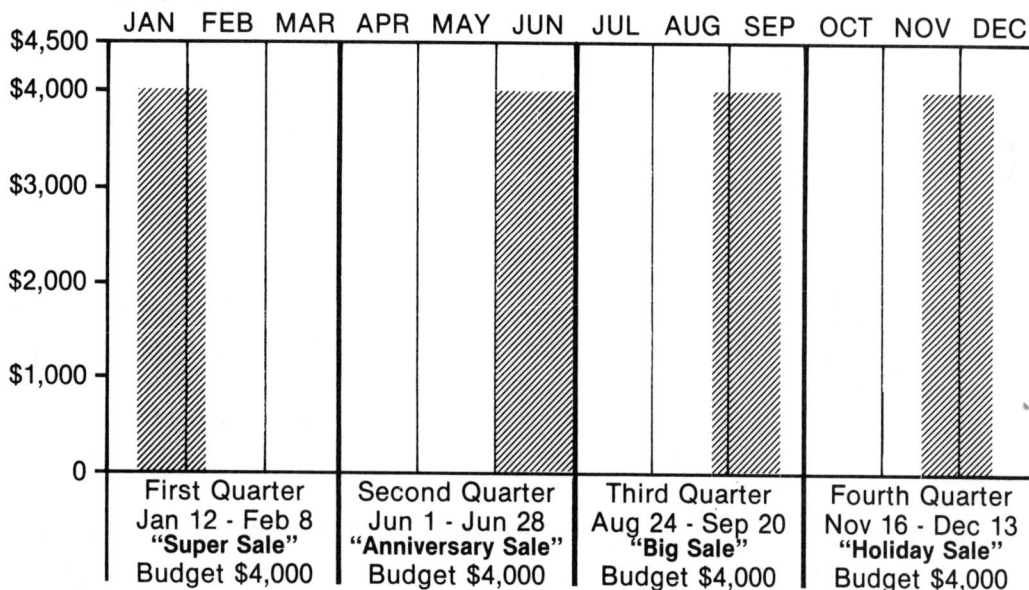

Four big sales at $4,000 each = $16,000 per year.

If you choose the "promotional sale" method of allocating your media dollars, you must first determine when and for what reason you are going to hold a big promotional sale. Make a list of the times of the year when it's most logical and beneficial for you to do so, i.e., Christmas season, back-to-school, your anniversary, January clearance, etc. You may evolve a list of ten logical times of the year for you to promote a sale. That's O.K., have ten "mini-promotions" instead of four "major promotions". The important thing is that you plan your sales events well in advance and allocate enough media dollars to them to be able to reach the buying public with your "customer benefits ladened" sales message.

If you allocated $4000 for your Christmas promotional budget, it would look something like this:

a. 1000 direct mailers to current customers announcing
private sale prior to start of the big sale   - $ XXX

b. 4 weeks of radio
   • Station a, 18 spots per week   - $ XXX
   • Station b, 18 spots per week   - $ XXX

c. 4 weeks of newspaper ads
   • newspaper a, 2-40" ads per week on Thursday
    and Friday   - $ XXX

d. Extra POP signs not allocated in regular
POP budget   -   <u>$ XXX</u>
   TOTAL CHRISTMAS PROMOTIONAL BUDGET   - $4000

3. Method C — Consistency with Promotions

I recommend this method. It combines the benefits of consistently keeping your sales message before the public with the advantages of holding three or four or more hard-hitting promotions per year. Your base-line or consistent advertising could be as simple as a weekly ad in Sunday's newspaper, or three spots per week on TV in the late news, or twelve spots per week on radio. Your three or four hard-hitting promotions would then be placed over your consistent advertising.

I've seen many variations of this philosophy. One retailer's annual advertising plan called for three weeks of "consistent advertising" averaging $300 per week and one week per month of "One Week Only Sale" advertising with media expenditures of $900 during that special week. At the end of the year he had run 36 weeks of "consistent advertising" at $300 per week ($10,800) and 12 weeks of "One Week Only Sale" advertising at $900 per promotion week ($10,800) for a total annual media expenditure of $21,600.

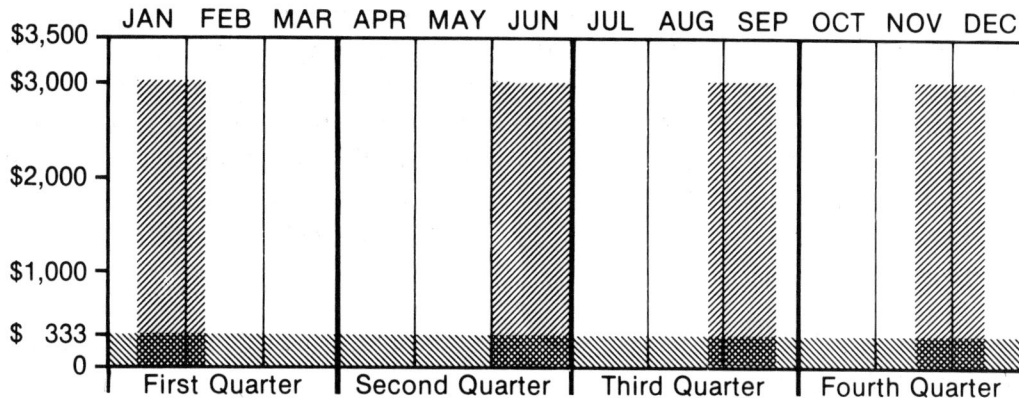

```
           JAN  FEB  MAR  APR  MAY  JUN  JUL  AUG  SEP  OCT  NOV  DEC
$3,500 ─
$3,000 ─
$2,000 ─
$1,000 ─
$  333 ─
     0 ─
           First Quarter   Second Quarter   Third Quarter   Fourth Quarter
```

Four sales at $3,000 each = $12,000
plus $333 per month =   3,996
For a total yearly budget of $15,996

Your annual advertising budget will dictate whether you have one promotional sale per month, one per quarter or one per year. The key point is to make your sale promotions as hard-hitting as possible. Make them strong so they'll attract attention and new customers. But, don't forget to use your "consistent weekly advertising" to motivate new customers also. Obviously, your "consistent advertising" will not be as strong as your "promotion advertising", but remember the purpose of all advertising is to SELL! Don't waste those weekly ads, thinking you're just keeping your name before the public waiting for your big sale promotion to roll around. Horse-feathers! **SELL, SELL, SELL. . .ALL THE TIME!!!**

You Can't Have Too Many Sales

Don't be afraid to promote a lot of "SALES". K-Mart, Radio Shack, Macy's, Sears, etc., have some kind of a sale every week. They realize that their "sale advertising" is only going to be noticed by a very small percentage of the market.

There are only X number of people during a given week who can be classified as "potential buyers of your product." It's a very small percentage. Maybe only 1% or less of the population of your city. That's who you're rifling your advertising message to. The problem is, you don't know who makes up that 1%, because it changes from week to week. 99 people out of 100 are going to totally ignore your advertising because they're simply not interested. They're not a part of that "potential buyers" category.

Let's say you're in the appliance business and my wife and I have decided to buy a microwave oven. We're potential buyers this week. We're looking at all the microwave oven ads. We're looking for the best buy. If you're running "a big sale on microwave ovens" we're going to notice your advertising and maybe buy your microwave oven. If we do, we're no longer potential buyers of a microwave oven. Next week we could care less about microwave oven ads. We've got ours. But we're going to be replaced by another couple who are now in the market for a mircowave oven and they're going to be looking at the sale ads and the process starts all over again.

The point I'm making is that there's nothing wrong with having a "Big Sale" every week of the year (if you could afford to do it) because the people who are going to pay attention to your "Big Sale" advertising are going to change from week to week.

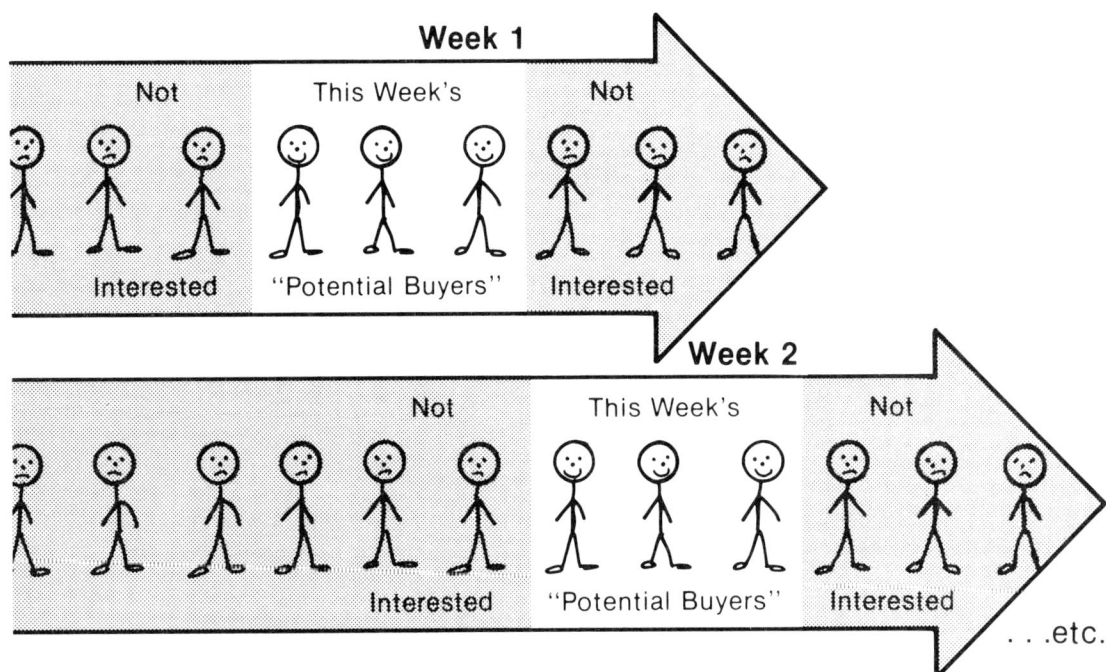

The small percentage of people who are in the "potential buyers category" changes from week to week. Your "sale advertising" will be noticed by them and ignored by everyone else. Each week introduces a new set of "potential buyers" and a new advertising opportunity for you.

In order to help you keep track of your monthly advertising expenditures, I've prepared a "Monthly Budget Summary" for you on the following two pages.

MONTHLY BUDGET SUMMARY

Date:_____   Budget for the Month of:_____

I. Media

A. Newspaper _____ # of Inches   Rate   Cost _____

   1. _____   _____   _____

   2. _____   _____   _____

   3. _____   _____   _____

   4. _____   _____   _____

                        Sub-Total Print _____

B. T.V. _____ # of Spots   Rate

   1. _____   _____   _____

   2. _____   _____   _____

   3. _____   _____   _____

                        Sub-Total T.V. _____

C. Radio _____ # of Spots   Rate

   1. _____   _____   _____

   2. _____   _____   _____

   3. _____   _____   _____

   4. _____   _____   _____

                        Sub-Total Radio _____

D. Other Adv. Programs   Description _____

   1. _____   _____

   2. _____   _____

   3. _____   _____

                        Sub-Total Other _____

                 I. Media Total for Month _____

II. Support Services

A. Fixed Advertising Costs   Cost

1. Yellow Pages   _____
2. Business Directory   _____
3.   _____
4.   _____
5.   _____

                                       Sub-Total Fixed _____

B. Point-of-Purchase Costs

1. POP Displays   _____
2. POP Signs   _____
3.   _____
4.   _____

                                           Sub-Total POP _____

C. Production Costs

1. Print Production   _____
2. Radio Production   _____
3. T.V. Production   _____
4.   _____
5.   _____
6.   _____

                             Sub-Total Production _____

         II. Support Services Total for Month _____

                         I. Media Total _____

         TOTAL AD BUDGET FOR MONTH _____

Advertising Agencies

Do you need an advertising agency?

If your answer to my question is, "What is an advertising agency?"... then you probably do not need one.

But, just in case your advertising budget is large enough and your advertising requirements complicated enough to require professional help, let's discuss the client/agency relationship so you'll know what to expect.

In simple terms, an advertising agency's function is to assist it's clients in planning, producing and placing the company's advertising.

Sounds easy enough, but look what's involved:

1. Planning

   A good agency is research oriented and will spend a lot of time producing relevent data to help you better understand your company's strengths and weaknesses. They will direct their efforts toward finding the answers to...Who are your potential customers? What are their buying habits? How can they be motivated? Once they obtain a knowledgeable insight into the personality of your company and your customer base, they will be in a position to help plan an advertising program to present your best image and strongest sales points to the greatest potential audience.

2. Production

   A good agency can provide creativity and knowledge of print production including layout, pasteup, finished art, illustration, photography, typesetting, etc. An agency can provide the creativity and knowledge of the numerous radio and TV production techniques available to produce effective radio and TV spots.

3. Media Placement

A good agency understands demographics, CPM's, GRP's, share, rating, target segmentation, reach, frequency and has the ability to negotiate the best possible rates. Effective media placement is an art and a science.

Advertising Agencies Are People

Larger professional advertising agencies have people on their staff who specialize in planning, production and placement. Their Personnel roster could read like this:

Account Supervisor — responsible for overall management of the account.

Account Executive — responsible for service and managing the account on a day-to-day basis. Communicates client's objectives to the agency and the agency's plan of action to the client.

Creative Director — creates and oversees the overall creative direction the client should take with his advertising.

Market Research Director — coordinates the research divisions of the agency.

Print Copywriter — writes copy for print campaigns.

Broadcast Copywriter — writes copy for radio and TV campaigns.

Art Director — oversees all areas involving graphics and coordinates all print campaigns.

Artist — prepares all print elements.

Radio and TV Director — produces radio and TV commercials.

Media Director — oversees all media planning and buying functions.

Media Buyer — negotiates with media reps and makes media buys.

In addition to those listed, you could also find additional production assistants, artists, media buyers, research analysts, photographers, public relations specialists, secretaries and accounting personnel. An agency's "inventory" walks into the office in the morning and leaves in the evening. The more creative, experienced and talented the people, the better the agency. A normal rule of thumb for an agency as far as staff is concerned is it takes four or five people (depending upon how multi-talented and efficient they are) to handle a million dollars in annual billings.

Annual Billings

The size of the agency is measured by annual billings. An agency billing one million dollars per year means the clients that agency represents spend one million dollars per year on radio, TV, newspaper, research, production, etc., through that agency.

"I work better under pressure."

Professional Consultants Vs. Unqualified Substitutes

I've heard numerous agencies make presentations to clients and refer to themselves as "professional consultants." They've drawn the analogy. . . "just as you seek the advice and counsel of your lawyer and doctor in legal and health matters, you need the guidance of an advertising agency in marketing and advertising matters."

Now I will agree that the majority of well-established, successful advertising agencies deserve to be called "professional consultants" and are as competent in their field as doctors and lawyers are in their chosen professions.

But, I must warn you there are some advertising agencies who are incompetent and have no right to call themselves "professional consultants" much less compare themselves to a doctor or lawyer. Doctors and lawyers spend many years in school, put in long, hard hours of post graduate study, obtain a degree and pass a state bar exam or medical exam to **earn the right** to call themselves doctors or lawyers. Anyone can open an advertising agency! Unfortunately for the industry, there are far too many unqualified, uneducated, inexperienced people calling themselves "advertising agencies". These are the so-called "advertising consultants" you should avoid. They are unqualified substitutes for the real thing. Let three or four agencies make a presentation to you and it won't take long to separate the actors from the qualified, legitimate advertising agencies.

Choosing An Agency

If your budget is less than $1700 per month (less than $20,000 per year), my advice is to study this manual in depth, put your program together, and administer it yourself. From $20,000 to $50,000 per year, depending on the nature of your account, availability of qualified agencies, and market conditions, you may benefit from the services of a good agency.

Over $50,000 per year in advertising expenditures definitely warrants an investigation of qualified agencies available in your area and what they can do for you. You can always go shopping without buying. Even if you don't find one you like, you'll benefit from the knowledge you'll acquire from interviewing three or four qualified agencies.

More than likely your advertising expenditures are not going to be sufficient enough to attract a large, multi-talented, multi-staffed regional advertising agency. You're going to have to spend some time looking for a local agency that's qualified to handle your advertising. But that's O.K. There are a lot of smaller agencies (even some one-man shops) in every market that are talented, sincere, well-qualified and professional in their business relationships.

When you start looking, here are some guidelines to follow:

1. Need

Before you decide to interview agencies, you've got to decide if you really need one. Sit down and review your entire advertising program from top to bottom.

a. Is your budget large enough to warrant using an agency?

b. What do you want an agency to do for you?

c. What can an agency do that you can't do for yourself?

d. How much time do you have to spend on your ad program? Can an agency take on some of the tasks you're now doing and free your time for other projects?

e. Do you take advice well? Are you willing to listen to qualified advice or will you end up doing it your way anyway?

f. What are your alternatives? Who can do your production? Who can help plan your ad program? Who can make your media buys? Who can conduct your research programs?

g. Do you enjoy doing your own advertising? Do you feel you're pretty creative and have a good advertising head on your shoulders? Will you miss working with the media reps, production people and suppliers?

2. Compatibility

A good agency/client relationship is like a good marriage. It's built on trust and clear communications. I don't care how talented an agency is, if you're not compatible, its not going to work.

3. Qualifications

Remember an agency is only as good as it's people, so ask the following questions to determine how qualified the agency is to handle your account:

a. How many people are involved in your agency? What are their responsibilities and their qualifications?

b. Who will be assigned to my account?

c. What accounts are you currently handling? Who is your biggest account? Your smallest?

d. May I see samples of your most recent campaigns for some of these accounts?

e. How long have you been in business?

f. What accounts have you lost during the past year? Why?

g. In which area of advertising do you feel your agency is strongest?

h. Of your total billings, please give the percentages in newspaper, radio, television, magazine, direct mail.

i. Who is responsible for the "creative" that comes out of your agency?

4. References

Request the names of five of the agency's accounts and the people they work with at those accounts. Ask permission to call and see what they have to say about the agency. Since they're currently working with the agency, they'll be the best judge of how good the agency is.

Next, call the sales managers at some of the local TV and radio stations and ask their opinion of the agency. Talk to the media credit managers and check out their credit.

5. Terms of Agreement

If you were to work with this agency, find out how they would want to be compensated for their services and what kind of agreement they require.

Fair Compensation

If you have determined you definitely need an agency and you have found one you feel can do the job for you, don't hesitate to pay them fairly for what they do.

Remember, an agency sells it's time, it's creative ability and it's experience. Agencies are normally compensated for their services in the following manner:

1. Media Placement

For selecting, placing, trafficking and verifying all media placements, they receive a 15% commission from the media. Where the media is not commissionable to the agency, the media costs are usually marked up to obtain the 15% commission.

2. Client Costs

All costs incurred on a client's behalf, i.e., printing, typesetting, talent charges, photography charges, etc., are billed to the client at cost, plus a markup usually around 20%. Some agencies and clients feel it's to their mutual advantage to work on a straight "fee" arrangement whereby the agency is paid a set monthly service fee and all client costs, including media purchases are billed net to the client.

3. Production Charges

Art hours required by the agency artist or art director to produce print ads, or broadcast production hours required by the agency's creative director to produce TV or radio spots are billed to the client at an agreed upon per hour rate that could range from $10 per hour to $60 per hour. Make sure you ask what the hourly charges are and the average time it takes to produce a broadcast commercial or print ad. You need to be assured that your budget won't be eaten up by service fees.

4. Approved in Advance

All costs, be it for media, production or research, should be clearly spelled out in advance, in detail and approved in writing by you. A copy of the approved budget should be compared to the actual billing to see if the agency is over or under budget. There should never be any hidden costs, or "oh, I forgot about that" charges.

If you are not willing to pay for the hours, don't demand the service. Your agency is in business to make a profit just like you and it cannot do that by giving away its services. You should receive value for value given.

Teamwork

Effective advertising is produced not only by great agencies, but by equally great clients working with them. Once you have selected an agency, your success will depend as much on how you treat them as how they treat you.

Remember, this is a marriage built on trust, communication, sharing and fairness. Treat your agency as an equal partner. Its job by definition is to represent you. Therefore, you have to share your strengths and weaknesses. . .your goals and aspirations. . .successes and failures. You must work as a team to build a mutually profitable relationship.

Advertising Results

The hardest question to answer for any advertiser is, "How do I measure the results of my advertising?" If sales are up 20% can you say it's because of your good advertising strategies? If I had not advertised at all, would I still have achieved my 20% increase in sales? If sales are down 20%, can you blame it on your advertising? Had I spent more money on advertising, could I have overcome my 20% drop in sales? What advertising worked for me and what advertising was a wasted investment? Every advertiser constantly wrestles with these questions.

The marketing process contains many variables. What motivates people to buy or not to buy? Economic conditions, the weather, human behavior, price, public opinion, quality, advertising and many other factors enter into the purchasing decision. All of the experts agree that we simply do not know enough about human behavior to explain why people buy certain products and not others. Nor would we be able to qualify this information in a precisely meaningful way, even if we could find out. The realities of the situation are, that accurately measuring advertising results cannot be done in a totally satisfactory manner.

But, this doesn't mean you shouldn't try to measure advertising results. Whether you work with an advertising agency or handle your own advertising, you should always **demand results from your advertising!**

Strive to know and document what works and what doesn't work. Create methods of measurement that will help you judge the effectiveness of your advertising programs. But don't be frustrated if you discover your answers are not totally conclusive. By constantly trying to measure your results, you'll reduce your uncertainty about certain types of advertising and at least acquire a "feel", if not factual information, for what works and what doesn't work.

If you would like to measure the consumer awareness of your advertising, you can do so by conducting a simple telephone survey.

Make 100 random telephone calls in your marketing area. If an adult answers the phone, tell him or her that you are conducting a research study and would they please answer 5 simple questions regarding advertising?

1. Of all the advertising you have seen, read or heard in the last 30 days, which comes first to mind?

   • more than likely you are going to receive an answer like "Coca-Cola" or "McDonald's" or "Pepsi-Cola". So your second question is aimed at getting the respondent to narrow his or her answer to the area that you're interested in.

2. Of all the advertising of **local advertisers** you have seen, read or heard in the last 30 days, which comes first to mind?

   • now you're starting to gather information that's more pertinent to what you want to know.

3. Of all the local **restaurant advertising** (or furniture store advertising or tire dealer advertising, use the proper category for the type of business you're in) you have seen, read or heard in the last 30 days, which comes first to mind?

   • this is the key question. You will be able to measure the awareness of your advertising in relation to the competition. If your business is given as the answer to question #3, then go directly to question #5. If not, then you're going to have to "assist" the respondent with question #4.

4. During the last 30 days, do you remember seeing, reading or hearing the advertising for (insert the name of your business)?

   • now you're aiding the respondent so you're no longer measuring the awareness level of your advertising. You're now trying to find out what forms of advertising you're using are working the best.

195

5. Where did you see, read or hear the (insert the name of your business) advertising?

  • try to get the respondent to be as specific as possible. If they say "radio", ask which radio station? If they say "TV", ask which TV program? etc.

"Thank you very much for taking the time to participate in our advertising awareness survey. Have a nice day."

The "awareness level" of your advertising is determined by tallying the unaided responses of the first three questions.

By analyzing the aided responses of the last two questions, you should be able to determine what forms of advertising (radio, TV, newspaper, etc.) are working best for you.

If you conduct this survey once every other month, or on a quarterly basis, you should be able to measure the awareness level of your advertising compared to the competition.

Now, what methods of measurement can you use internally to judge the effectiveness of your advertising program?

1. The Cash Register

   This is where it counts. Are your sales going up or going down? Attempting to use sales to measure the effectiveness of your advertising can be tricky because there is not always a direct cause-and-effect relationship between the two. But whenever possible, try to relate your advertising efforts to sales.

2. Sourcing

   Some retailers make it a normal part of every sale to ask the buyer, "What motivated you to shop here?" Some retailers even have the various sources noted on the sales slip, i.e., newspaper ad, TV spot, radio station WXYZ, recommended by a friend, etc. If you have a detailed questionnaire, you'll be able to compile a more accurate analysis of what advertising is working and what's not working.

3. Word-of-mouth

It's always nice to hear, "I saw your advertising and thought I'd give you a try." But the majority of people are hesitant to volunteer information like that. However, with a little coaxing and some friendly conversation, you'll be able to illicit some comments about your advertising from your customers.

4. Coupons

All forms of printed coupon advertising provide you with the opportunity to measure the effectiveness of your advertising by the number of coupons redeemed compared to the cost of running the ad.

5. Item and price advertising

If you feature certain items on sale at a special advertised price, your success ratio is in direct proportion to the number of featured items you sell. If you have a special one-day, one-week or one-month sale and advertise numerous items at special prices, then you will know at the end of this event whether you had a successful sales promotion or a failure.

6. Contests

If you sponsor a contest and promote that contest as part of your advertising program, you'll be able to measure the success of your advertising by the number of entries you receive compared to the cost of running the promotion.

7. Premiums

How many times have you seen free premium items offered to encourage store traffic, "drop in today for your free calendar", "come visit us at our new location and pick up your copy of our free cook book"? The number of people responding to your offer provides some measurement of the success of your advertising. In some cases, the advertising is unique enough that **it** becomes the premium item people request. This happened with a series of full-page ads United Technologies ran in the Wall Street Journal that motivated 91,061 letters and requests for 458,667 reprints. The following pages are reprints of two of twelve similar ads that appeared in the Wall Street Journal. Naturally, I was attracted to this first ad because of the headline, "Keep It Simple". I love it!

SECTION SIX REVIEW NOTES

Let's review what we talked about in the sixth section:

1. You need to take three elements into consideration in structuring your advertising plan:

    a. Your objective

    b. Your strategy

    c. Your specific recommendations

2. In structuring your annual plan, make sure you identify where the dollars are being spent. How mcuh are you actually spending on:

    a. Reaching and motivating new customers

    b. "Back-up" support services

3. At least 60% or more of your budget should go toward reaching and motivating new customers.

4. Three possible approaches to structuring your advertising plan are:

    a. Consistent monthly expenditures

    b. Strategically placed promotions

    c. Consistency with promotions

5. An advertising agency can help you in planning, producing and placing your advertising.

6. Your annual budget, organizational structure, and need will determine if you should interview qualified agencies.

7. A successful agency/client relationship is a teamwork effort.

8. The hardest question to answer for any advertiser is, "How do I measure the results of my advertising?"

9. The realities of the situation are that accurately measuring advertising results cannot be done in a **totally** satisfactory manner. But in spite of measurement limitations you should always **demand results from your advertising!**

10. There are various methods of measurement:

   a. Sales

   b. Sourcing

   c. Word-of-mouth

   d. Couponing

   e. Item-and-price advertising

   f. Contests

   g. Premiums

   h. Telephone surveys

"Bill, I think I've found our bottleneck."

HELPFUL INFORMATION ...from the AD PLANNER

Here are the steps I'm going to take to. . .

1. Get My House in Order
   a.

   b.

   c.

2. Identify My Target Customers
   a.

   b.

   c.

3. Determine My Advertising Budget
   a.

   b.

   c.

4. Establish My Creative Approach
   a.

   b.

   c.

5. Review All My Media Possibilities
   a.

   b.

   c.

6. Explore My Production Possibilities

    a.

    b.

    c.

7. Establish My PR and Community Relations Programs

    a.

    b.

    c.

8. Organize My Annual Advertising Plan

    a.

    b.

    c.

9. Plan, Produce, and Place My Advertising

    a.

    b.

    c.

10. Measure the Results of My Advertising Efforts

    a.

    b.

    c.

DICTIONARY OF ADVERTISING TERMS

Crain Books publishes and offers numerous books on advertising including "Successful Direct Marketing Methods", "A Technique for Producing Ideas", and a "Dictionary of Advertising Terms". You can write to them at 740 Rush Street, Chicago, IL 60611, and they will send you a FREE catalog listing of their publications.

With their permission, I would like to share some advertising word definitions taken from a "Dictionary of Advertising Terms", published by Tatham-Laird & Kudner, edited by Laurence Urdand and offered by Crain Books:

advertise · to attempt to persuade people to voluntarily produce a recommended behavior pattern by presenting them with an openly sponsored, multiply reproduced message; the message is delivered by purchased use of a medium's space or time.

affidavit of performance · a notarized statement from a television or radio station that a message or program was presented as ordered.

affordable method · a method for determining marketing budgets based on use of judgment as to what is affordable after other spending and profit goals are established.

agate line · a unit of space calculated for advertising sales purposes; equal to 1/14 inch in depth by one standard column in width.

agency commission · a commission paid by a communications medium, as a television or radio station or a periodical, to an advertising agency, usually in the form of a 15% discount on the gross advertising rate billed to a client by the agency.

aided recall · a measure of recall of an advertisement or series of advertisements by a test respondent who has been aided by prompting.

air · to broadcast (a television or radio commercial or program).

animation · the creation of an effect of movement, life, or human character to a representation of an object, animal, or person. This may be done by means of a series of cartoons.

annual discount · a discount given by a print or broadcast medium to an advertiser who purchases fifty-two consecutive weeks of space or time.

art and mechanical · noting or pertaining to graphic materials required for production of an advertisement.

attitude study · a survey of attitudes toward an organization, product, service, etc., as expressed in the answers of respondents to questions; often made before and after an advertising campaign or the like to determine change of attitude.

audience profile · a digest of the relevant characteristics of the typical audience of a communications medium, such as age, family size, income, or location; used to evaluate the suitability of the medium for specific kinds of advertising.

average audience rating · (in television or radio) a rating based on the number of persons tuned in to a program compared with some basic figure, e.g., the number the program is able to reach; calculated by averageing a series of ratings made at intervals over a brief period of time.

average net paid circulation · the average circulation of a periodical per issue, established by dividing the total number of copies sold for the period being examined by the number of issues during the period.

bait advertising · advertising that offers a sale item at a low price to entice buyers, although the cost of an actual purchase is intended to be higher.

banner · a display poster for retail advertising, especially one draped over a wire or cord so as to be readable from both sides.

barter · the furnishing of products by an advertiser as full or partial payment for spot broadcasting time or free mentions.

best time available · schedule an advertiser's commercial, at the broadcast station's discretion, in the best available commercial occasion; a scheduling instruction for television or radio advertising.

billing · a flat, upright structure for the display of outdoor advertising.

bleed · to print an illustration so that it goes to the very edge of a page on one or more sides, without a border or margin.

blueline · a proof of offset printing work, made on photosensitive paper and typically blue.

boldface · any printing type whose strokes and serifs are thicker than those normal for its font; used to call attention to certain words without an increase in type size.

bonus spot · a television or radio advertising occasion offered gratis by a station as a means to increase a sponsor's gross rating points or as a bonus for the purchase of a package.

brochure · a booklet whose appearance has been given special design attention, and that has often been bound in special cover stock.

burried advertisement · surrounded by other advertising so as to be inconspicuous.

buyout · a one-time payment to television or radio talent for all rights to performance.

campaign · a program of coordinated advertisements and promotional activities, intended to accomplish specific sales objectives.

center spread · the two facing pages at the center of a periodical, desirable because the pages are continuous, with little or no interruption at the gutter.

chain break · a network affiliated station's interruption of network broadcasting for local station identification.

circular · a printed advertising sheet mailed, inserted in packages, or distributed by hand.

clutter · the number of advertisements claiming the attention of the audience of a television or radio program.

collateral · advertising material other than that presented through communications media.

color separations · a set of black and white color separation negatives of full color or copy made through the use of color filters for transformation into color printing plates; these commonly represent the yellow, red and blue tones, and are often combined with a black plate to enrich the shadow values.

column · an area of print running down a page of a periodical, composed of lines of equal width.

column inch · a unit of space one standard column wide and one inch deep; in newspaper publishing, this is 14 agate lines deep.

commercial time · a standard amount of time and number of interruptions which television and radio broadcasters who are members of NAB are permitted to devote to non-program material.

commercial protection · a time interval preceding and following an advertiser's commercial that a broadcaster customarily or contractually keeps free of commercials for competitive products or services.

composition · the setting of type according to a customer's requirements; the arrangements of the various elements of an advertisement.

consumer survey · a survey of public attitudes, buying habits, etc., especially one done among the actual or potential customers of a consumer product.

continuous tone · noting or pertaining to photographs or the like that have continuous shading rather than shading rendered with halftone dots, hatching, etc.

cooperative advertising · advertising run by a local advertiser in cooperation with a national advertiser, the latter usually supplying the copy, plates, or reproduction materials; the two share both the cost and the mention of their names.

copyright · to register a writing, work of art, design, etc., with the Library of Congress upon publication in order to establish one's exclusive right to reproduce the material in question.

cost efficiency · the effectiveness of an advertising medium measured with reference to its actual or potential audience and its cost for advertising placement (usually expressed in cost per thousand).

cost per gross rating point · a measure of broadcast media efficiency of particular use to media planners; represents the price of a single gross rating point for a medium.

cost per thousand · the advertising cost required to reach one thousand persons, homes, or other audience units. With periodicals, the advertising rate or actual advertisement cost is divided by the circulation, interpreted as the estimated number of readers or ad-noters. With television and radio, the rate charged for commercial placement is divided by the average number of persons or homes tuned in.

creative strategy · a statement of the communications goal and basic message (not specific content) to be used in an advertisement, or series of advertisements; usually consists of a stated intent, target prospect description, the benefit or benefits to be promised, and the facts to be used to support the believability of the benefits promised.

cross merchandising · displaying of related retail items in alternate order, as one opposite sides of a supermarket aisle; done so that a customer in search of one item may buy another on impulse.

cumulative audience · a television or radio audience, computed either individuals or homes, that views or listens to some portion of a series of programs or commercials.

daypart · any of the time segments into which the broadcasting day of a television or radio station is divided.

defensive spending · expenditures for marketing activities intended to protect an established business from competitive inroads.

direct response advertising · advertising which attempts to obtain orders for purchase to be made directly to the manufacturer or servicer, rather than through agents, stores, or other dealers.

discount · any reduction from a stated price or rate of payment, made for various reasons. An advertiser may receive a discount, for instance, for purchasing a certain large quantity of space or time in a communications medium; an advertising agency receives much of its revenue in the form of discounts from media on billings to advertisers; a retailer buys from a wholesaler at a discount from the established retail price.

discrepancy · an incongruity between two related things, as media space or time ordered and that billed to the advertiser.

dub · to blend sound into the previously recorded sound track of a film, or audio or video tape.

duotone · a two-color printing process for enriching the effect of black and white halftone illustration printing by adding an additional color from a second halftone plate, in register, using a different screen angle.

earned rate · the actual rate for advertising space or time charged to an advertiser, taking into account all discounts for volume and frequency.

efficiency · advertising audience size in comparison with the cost of placing the advertising; usually expressed as a cost-per-thousand exposed audience units.

fixed position · a specific period of station broadcasting time reserved for an advertiser and sold at a premium rate.

flight saturation · maximum concentration of spot television or radio advertising within a short period, to a point at which any further advertising would presumably have diminishing or negative effects.

format · the size of a book or periodical page described as folio, quarto, etc., according to the number of pages in a signature; the general design of a book or periodical page, or piece of graphic art.

fragmentation · use of a great variety of types of media for a single advertising campaign, with no single medium used predominantly, or heavily.

freelance · to work independently, being paid by the job.

frequency discount · a discount to an advertiser for running a certain number of advertisements within a specified period.

gross impression · the sum of all exposures to an advertiser's advertising in a given media schedule.

gross rating point · a unit of measurement of television, radio, or outdoor advertising audience size, equal to 1% of the total potential audience universe; used to measure the exposure of one or more programs or commercials, without regard to multiple exposure of the same advertising to individuals.

halftone screen · a screen through which a photograph is taken to make a halftone negative.

hiatus · a temporary interruption of a sponsored program, typically during the 8 to 13 weeks of the summer season; a temporary cessation of advertising schedules, as between flights.

hook · any device in a printed advertisement intended to stimulate an immediate response or inquiry.

illustrator · a person who uses nonphotographic means, such as paint, ink, or pencil, to create pictures for use in advertisements.

impact · the effect of a communications medium on its audience.

impulse buy · a consumer purchase motivated by chance rather than plan.

indicia · an envelope marking accepted by a postal service in lieu of stamps on bulk mailings.

investment spending · increased advertising or promotion expenditures for a product or service, typically funded by temporary reductions in the profit rate in the expectation of future increases in sales and profits.

jingle · music and verse combined in a commercial; typically sung, and usually characterized by a compelling rhyme scheme.

keyline · an arrangement of all typographic and visual elements of an advertisement, brochure, mailer, etc., showing precisely the size and position of each element; normally with reproduction type proofs in position, as well as photostats of illustrations showing size and positioning.

Likert scale · a summated scale for attitude measurement in which respondents state their agreement or disagreement with statements in one of a range of three to seven possible positions, ranging from complete agreement, to no opinion, to complete disagreement.

lineage · a total amount of periodical advertising space, named in the number of lines run.

local rate · the advertising rate charged by a local communications medium to a local advertiser; usually lower than the national rate.

logotype · a brand name, publication title, or the like, presented in a special lettering style or typeface and used in the manner of a trademark.

margin · the difference between cost and selling price of a product; computed either as a cash figure or as a percentage of the selling price.

marketing · the knowledge and active processes of a seller directed to fulfillment of gainful exchanges; such processes include product or service development, pricing, packaging, advertising, merchandising, and distribution.

mat service · a service that supplies newspapers with matrixes of advertising, artwork, public relations material, etc.

merchandising · marketing activities, including sales and promotion, designed to make retail goods available, attractive and conspicuous in a store.

minimum frequency · a level of exposure to or, scheduling of advertising that is believed to represent the lowest level at which the advertising will be effective in attaining its ends, while permitting the greatest degree of advertising continuity.

net rating point · a single percent of the total potential audience, unduplicated; used in expressing a net rating.

net unduplicated audience · the actual number of persons who may be exposed to advertising, regardless of how many exposures each person may have.

Nielsen rating · a rating of television program audience size used by the A.C. Nielson Co., stated in terms of gross ratings points either for those who have heard the program for the average minute in a quarter hour, or those who have been exposed to the program for five or more minutes.

one-time rate · the rate charge for a single, unrepeated advertisement.

pasteup · an assemblage of type proofs, art work, etc., pasted on paperboard, used for reproduction by an engraver or printer.

penetration · the effectiveness of advertising in reaching and persuading the public.

percentage-of-sales method · a method for determining marketing budgets based on a predetermined percentage rate of spending relative to anticipated dollar sales.

photocomposition · non-metal typographic machine composition using characters on photographic grids to produce letterform images on photographic film or paper.

Photostat · a type of high contrast photographic negative or positive made on paper.

plate · a flat sheet of material, flexible or rigid, made of metal or plastic, whose surface will accept an image capable of being reproduced by ink onto another surface, such as paper.

point-of-purchase · the place at which a customer encounters a retail item that he may buy.

preempt · to take precedence with regard to television or radio time regardless of prior commitments.

preferred position · a location for an advertisement in a periodical or television or radio schedule that an advertiser demands and for which he is charged a higher than usual rate.

preprint · a printing of periodical advertising matter on separate sheets before actual publication; done by an advertiser for special purposes, e.g., to serve as retail displays or in order to merchandise his advertising support to retailers.

promotion · a usually temporary effort to create extra interest in the purchase of a product or service by offering values in excess of those customarily afforded by such purchases; includes temporary discounts, allowances premium offers, coupons, contests, sweepstakes, etc.

public relations · activities of persons or organizations intended to promote understanding of and good will toward themselves or their products or services.

qualitative research · research involving differences of kind or condition rather than of amount or degree; usually used to broaden insight and develop hypotheses.

quantitative research · statistical research involving differences of amount or degree rather than kind or condition; usually used to reach conclusions.

rate protection · guarantee of continuation at a former rate, made to an advertiser having a contract with a communications medium that raises its rates while the contract is in effect.

rating · any figure establishing the popularity of a television or radio program or the exposure obtained by the advertising it carries, usually measured as a percentage of the homes able to receive a program that actually do receive it.

reach and frequency · a criterion for evaluating the level of cumulative audience exposure of an advertising effort on the basis of the percentage of all persons or households who are exposed to the advertising (reach), and the average number of exposures for each (frequency), over a stated period of time. Gross rating points are equal to the product of reach and frequency.

regional edition · an edition of a national periodical distributed within one geographical area; its advertising space can be purchased separately.

representative sample · a form of quota sample in which percentages of various elements of a population are included that are regarded as representative of the whole population.

residual · a royalty paid to a performer or other person by a television or radio station or advertiser for a broadcast of a program or commercial; rates usually as established by union contract.

reverse · a photographic print in which values are inverted from the state in which they appear on a negative, as white type reversed out of a dark background.

run-of-schedule · the status of a television or radio announcement for which a specific day, or a specific hour, has not been reserved.

scatter plan · a broadcast advertising media plan calling for a series of advertising announcements presented at random during a number of television or radio programs.

segment · an identifiable subgroup of purchases or consumers within a market who share a common characteristic or special need.

self-mailer · a direct-mail piece folded and printed in such a way that no envelope or wrapper is required for mailing.

slogan · a sentence or phrase used consistently in a series of advertisements to express the central message.

spot announcement · (in television or radio) a commercial broadcast carried by an individual station, rather than a network.

standard newspaper · a newspaper of the standard size, normally 21½" in depth, 14½" wide, with eight columns totaling 2400 agate lines, or six columns totaling 1800 agate lines.

superimpose · to place over, as one camera image on another so as to create a composite image.

target market · an occupational, demographic, or psychographic group of consumers designated by a marketer as his best prospects for sales, and hence serves as the group at whom the marketer's most intensive sales, advertising, and promotional efforts are directed.

Velox · (trademark) a photographic print that is sometimes screened so that it can be rephotographed and reproduced as line copy.

waste circulation · a figure reflecting the readers of a periodical who are unlikely to purchase a certain product or service advertised in it.